MAKING TEACHING AND LEARNING VISIBLE

MAKING TEACHING AND LEARNING VISIBLE
COURSE PORTFOLIOS AND THE PEER REVIEW OF TEACHING

Daniel Bernstein
University of Kansas

Amy Nelson Burnett
Amy Goodburn
Paul Savory
University of Nebraska–Lincoln

ANKER PUBLISHING COMPANY, INC.

Published by Jossey-Bass
A Wiley Imprint
989 Market Street, San Francisco, CA 94103-1741   www.josseybass.com

Readers should be aware that Internet Web sites offered as citations and/or sources for further information may have changed or disappeared between the time this was written and when it is read.

Jossey-Bass books and products are available through most bookstores. To contact Jossey-Bass directly call our Customer Care Department within the U.S. at 800-956-7739, outside the U.S. at 317-572-3986, or fax 317-572-4002.

Jossey-Bass also publishes its books in a variety of electronic formats. Some content that appears in print may not be available in electronic books.

Library of Congress Cataloging-in-Publication Data

Making teaching and learning visible : course portfolios and the peer
    review of teaching / Daniel Bernstein ... [et al.].
        p. cm.
    Includes bibliographical references and index.
    ISBN-13: 978-1882982-96-7
    ISBN-10: 1-882982-96-7
    1. College teachers—Rating of. 2. College teaching. 3. Peer review.
4. Portfolios in education. I. Bernstein, Daniel.
LB2333.M27 2006
378.1'21—dc22   2006001698

Printed in the United States of America
FIRST EDITION
HB Printing   10 9 8 7 6 5 4 3 2 1

TABLE OF CONTENTS

LIST OF EXHIBITS

ABOUT THE AUTHORS

Daniel Bernstein is professor of psychology and director of the Center for Teaching Excellence at the University of Kansas. His effort in establishing and formalizing faculty peer review began in 1994 with his attendance at a conference sponsored by the American Association for Higher Education. He teaches courses in the history of psychology, learning and motivation, and social psychology. His research work focuses on adult motivation and learning in children. In 1998, Dr. Bernstein was a fellow in the Carnegie Academy for the Scholarship of Teaching and Learning; he was a charter member of the University of Nebraska–Lincoln (UNL) Academy of Distinguished Teachers; and in 2002 he received the Outstanding Teaching and Instructional Creativity Award from UNL. He earned his Ph.D. from the University of California–San Diego in 1973, and he taught psychology at UNL before joining the faculty at Kansas in the summer of 2002.

Amy Nelson Burnett is professor of history at the University of Nebraska–Lincoln (UNL). She received her Ph.D. in early modern history from the University of Wisconsin–Madison in 1989. Since 2000, she has co-coordinated UNL's Peer Review of Teaching Project. She is the author of *Teaching the Reformation: Ministers and their Message in Basel, 1529–1629* (Oxford University Press, 2006) and *The Yoke of Christ: Martin Bucer and Christian Discipline* (Truman State University Press, 1994), as well as numerous articles and essays on the Protestant Reformation in south Germany and Switzerland. She is the recipient of a research fellowship from the Alexander von Humboldt Foundation and has taught at the University of Hannover in Germany. In 1999, she received a College of Arts and Sciences Distinguished Teaching Award.

Amy Goodburn is associate dean of the College of Arts and Sciences and associate professor of English and women's studies at the University of Nebraska–Lincoln (UNL), where she teaches courses in writing, rhetoric, and literacy studies. Since 2001, she has co-coordinated UNL's Peer Review of Teaching Project. Her research focuses on ethnographic and teacher research, multicultural pedagogies, and curriculum development. Her recent edited collection is *Composition, Pedagogy, and the Scholarship of Teaching* (Boynton/Cook, 2002). Her contributions to teaching have been recognized by a College of Arts and Sciences Distinguished Teaching Award, UNL's Scholarly Teaching Award, and induction into UNL's Academy of Distinguished Teachers.

Paul Savory is associate professor in the Department of Industrial and Management Systems Engineering at the University of Nebraska–Lincoln (UNL). He earned his Ph.D. from Arizona State University in 1993. His teaching and research interests include engineering education, discrete-event computer simulation, engineering management, statistics, and operations research. Since 2000, he has co-coordinated UNL's Peer Review of Teaching Project. He has received numerous department, college, and university awards for his teaching effectiveness with the most recent being the 2004 Hollings Family Master Teacher Award for the College of Engineering. In 2003, he was inducted into the UNL Academy of Distinguished Teachers.

FOREWORD

It is hard to imagine a more exciting time to be a college or university teacher. This is not, of course, to say that teaching is easy in today's educational environment. Students bring a dizzying range of backgrounds and preparation to their work as learners. On many campuses, questions abound about what knowledge and skills are most important. Resources are scarce just about everywhere. And while technology offers new opportunities, it brings new puzzles and frustrations as well. Yet now more than ever, teaching presents faculty with exciting intellectual challenges, opportunities to collaborate with colleagues, and possibilities for both learning from and contributing to the work of others who care deeply about student learning. As this volume makes clear, growing numbers of faculty are seizing these opportunities and finding real rewards in doing so.

It is useful to retrace some of the developments that brought us to this exciting time. In the late 1980s, attention turned to the character of faculty work. From outside academe came calls for greater attention to the teaching of undergraduates, which was seen as neglected in the face of research interests and ambitions. But within the academy, too, surveys indicated that faculty valued their work as teachers and wanted to see greater balance between teaching and research. Boyer's (1990) work gave further focus and momentum to this idea, spreading a vision of scholarship that included not only basic research but teaching as well.

Over the subsequent decade, many campuses undertook examinations of faculty roles and rewards, seeking ways to bring greater recognition to teaching. Many of them established teaching centers to support serious work by faculty interested in exploring new classroom approaches. National projects, often with external funding, created significant momentum around some of these new approaches: learning communities, problem-based learning, collaborative learning, to name just a few. And the number of conferences, workshops, networks, and publications for capturing and exchanging ideas about teaching and learning was steadily on the rise. Many faculty were attracted to the idea of teaching as scholarly work and rallied around the growing movement for a scholarship of teaching and learning.

With this growing sense that teaching should be given greater attention and reward came a recognition that peer review—the central practice for evaluating scholarship in the disciplines—could usefully be applied to teaching as well. Recommendations to that effect began to appear in campus documents and reports, and in 1994 the American Association for Higher Education (AAHE) launched a four-year project (in which we were both involved) to explore new models for faculty to share and examine one another's instructional practice. Seeking to break out of a narrow definition of peer review as a "parachute drop" in which a senior colleague or administrator lands in one's classroom, checklist at the ready, the AAHE project generated an extensive menu of strategies for peer collaboration and review of teaching that put responsibility for educational quality much more squarely in faculty's hands. One of the institutions participating in that project was the University of Nebraska–Lincoln, and one of the strategies that emerged from the work was the course portfolio. Fast forward, then, to *Making Teaching and Learning Visible: Course Portfolios and the Peer Review of Teaching*, where the "marriage," as the authors call it, of peer review of teaching and the course portfolio is consummated, and its many fruits set forth for others to adopt and build on.

As illustrated by the stories of faculty featured in these pages, the course portfolio is an appealing peer review strategy for a number of reasons. First, it offers a way to make visible the intellectual work of teaching, work which is otherwise all too often lost. Along the way, the *process* of developing and sharing portfolios opens a door to collaboration—something many faculty welcome but have not experienced. Portfolios are also a way to bring greater rewards to teaching—by putting forward for peer review the hard work of course design, implementation, outcomes, and reflection. What is also clear is the variety of purposes served by the peer review. Some faculty are seeking feedback from close colleagues who can inform their efforts in a subsequent semester, while others are motivated by the need to see teaching represented more authentically—and persuasively—in promotion and tenure materials. Some are interested primarily in documenting what happens in the "target course"; others are actively investigating a research question about what works and why.

Regardless of purpose, what is clear is that the process of engagement with peer review portfolios is a valuable one. It is one that the authors lay out in a blueprint that is both detailed and flexible, illustrating each step along the way, and anticipating, as good teachers do, the possible obstacles and objections that may be encountered. They also offer a wide variety of examples across an array of disciplines—engineering, graphic design, English, history, political science, and art, to name just a few of the fields represented. In short, even those wholly new to peer review and course portfolios will be well prepared to move ahead by the guidance provided here.

But, as its title suggests, *Making Teaching and Learning Visible: Course Portfolios and the Peer Review of Teaching* is not simply a how-to resource. While much of the volume is taken up with practical matters, and the tone is often modest, the work reported here is animated by an ambitious vision and a bold set of values about the need for greater attention to teaching and—this is the real message of the book and its most important contribution—the imperative to look more closely at students' learning. As one of the book's authors has written elsewhere:

> By presenting examples of student work, teachers shift the focus of conversation from presentation style to learning and understanding. In writing and reflecting, each teacher articulates what has been effective in promoting learning and can use those insights to improve. By sharing work with peers, teachers are able to get helpful feedback from colleagues that can strengthen their work. (Bernstein & Wert, 2004)

This fine book carries a radical message, but its radicalism is not of the fist-banging, hand-wringing type. Nor is its rhetoric of crisis and emergency. Rather, the vision it offers is of a gradual process of transformation in which faculty develop, refine, and spread a new set of habits for strengthening and ensuring student learning. As one participant put it, once engaged in the reflection and exchange made possible by course portfolios, "you can't stop." It is, says another, "habit forming." Those who join forces with the faculty whose work is reported in the pages that follow will be joining in a journey toward serious cultural change, bringing teaching more fully to the center of academic life and reminding us that learning is, after all, higher education's highest calling.

Pat Hutchings, Vice President
Carnegie Foundation for the Advancement of Teaching

Ellen Wert, Director of Publications
Teacher Education Accreditation Council

Acknowledgments

The work described in this book represents a decade of sustained and focused effort by many people. While we served in coordinating and leading roles, the contributions of others made all this possible. It is ultimately their work that is worth reading and thinking about.

The project began when Interim Chancellor Joan Leitzel committed the University of Nebraska–Lincoln (UNL) to participating in the Peer Review of Teaching Project initiated by the American Association for Higher Education (AAHE). AAHE president Russ Edgerton partnered with Pat Hutchings and Lee Shulman in conceiving the project, and their collective practices formed the basis of our work. Their core of excellent ideas continues to drive this project.

Four critical sources of financial support allowed the work to grow until its own merit was established. The first wave of support came from the Fund for the Improvement of Postsecondary Education (FIPSE), and we benefited directly from the energy and ideas of the FIPSE director, Buddy Karelis. The University of Nebraska Foundation's Pepsi quasi-endowment fund provided the matching funds for the FIPSE grant and then provided bridging and matching funds for later grants. The Hewlett Foundation supported features of the data collection intended to evaluate the impact of the university's general education program. The Pew Charitable Trusts supported the full development of electronic course portfolios and the exchange of this intellectual work among five universities. Russ Edgerton supported this development from his position at the Trusts, and Ellen Wert provided outstanding guidance and many important insights in her role as our Pew grant officer.

Several academic leaders at UNL took the initiative to promote this project and help it find both financial and community support. Nancy Stara provided a steady stream of excellent ideas for implementing and institutionalizing the work and guided the hunt for external financial support. David Brinkerhoff was unwavering in finding appropriate matching funds to keep the initiative going. Rick Edwards gave vision to the project and provided a public forum for hard discussions about the best way to represent teaching in the academy. These three administrators were true leaders in giving our project the momentum it needed to become established in the UNL community.

Their successors, Barbara Couture and Dave Wilson, have continued to give active administrative support to the project financially and by promoting its visibility on campus.

At many stages in our evolution from peer collaboration to peer review, we benefited from the UNL Teaching and Learning Center and the Academic Senate's Teaching Council. Teaching and Learning Center director Delivee Wright provided support for our activities, and Laurie Bellows gave us invaluable insights into the perceptions of the faculty participants. The Teaching Council gave funds for faculty members to participate in the early versions of the program. Jessica Jonson, university-wide assessment coordinator added excellent guidance in framing the peer commentaries on course portfolios and in the evaluation of the impact of our program on student performance. During the externally funded phases of the project, the UNL psychology department provided needed space and invaluable logistical support. John Berman, Claudia Price-Decker, David Hansen, Cathy Oslzly, and Ardis Burkholder all contributed to our work by making us welcome in psychology and providing key skills we needed to keep the operation going. We also took great advantage of the outstanding skills of other psychology department members who worked on the project over a 10-year period. Marc Kiviniemi brought much-needed order to our planning and budgeting, and Karen Smith devised a thoughtful evaluation plan that guided our data collection. We required interaction with faculty members across campus, and we were fortunate that Joyce Schmeeckle, April Haberyan, Oksana Bendus, Yelena Kosheleva, Stacey Hoffman, Lesa Hoffman, Kathryn Kimbro, Ruth Casper, Michelle Oja, Lou Laguna, and Whitney Douglas had great skill in working with faculty members in generating their writing. A special thanks goes to Emily Springfield for her work in developing our initial project web site and in helping define the process and methods for creating electronic representations of faculty course portfolios.

Over the last several years we have had the privilege of working with many outstanding teachers at UNL as they have written their course portfolios. We especially want to thank Stu Bernstein, Dana Fritz, Kathy Krone, Chris Marvin, Nancy Miller, Wendy Smooth, LeenKiat Soh, and Tim Wentz for allowing us to highlight their work. Portions of Nancy Miller's course portfolio are reprinted by permission of the International Textile and Apparel Association.

We have also enjoyed our interactions with partners at four other universities who joined us in the last several years of the funded project. Faculty members at Kansas State University were among the earliest to recognize the potential of peer collaboration and review of teaching, and they engaged richly in the conversations that peer review can generate. Steve Kiefer, Ann Stalheim-Smith, and Betsy Cauble have been constant sources of collaborative work. At Indiana University, Jennifer Meta Robinson and Simon Brassell united to carry out the project and provide feedback to us on our procedures and plans. At the University of Michigan, Connie Cook, Matt Kaplan, and Crisca Bierwert guided the participation of Michigan faculty members and provided many interesting suggestions for the overall project. At Texas A&M University, Nancy Simpson led a very able group of faculty, with leadership from Bruce Dickson and Roger Smith.

Finally, we would like to dedicate this book to the memory of Al Kilgore, professor of education at UNL and assistant vice chancellor for academic affairs. It was Al who took Chancellor Leitzel's invitation to participate in peer review seriously, and he worked tirelessly to promote the notion that teaching is important intellectual work. He took the lead in creating the UNL Academy of Distinguished Teachers and pushed and prodded us as individuals to attempt work that seemed at odds with the institutional culture. Without his vision, support, and warm personal model, none of this work would have been undertaken. Al is sorely missed by his colleagues at UNL.

1 MAKING TEACHING AND LEARNING VISIBLE

How can a faculty member make visible the careful, difficult, and intentional scholarly work of planning and teaching a course? Consider the following three scenarios.

Scenario One: Office of your department chair, where you are having your annual merit review.

Your chair begins, "From your student teaching evaluations, it appears your students really like you." You nod, pleased at the affirmation, and she continues, "Also, from my two visits to your classroom this past year, it seems you have a good rapport with the students. So, overall, I'm rating you 'very good' in teaching. Now let's move on and talk about your research."

In comparison to her brief discussion of your teaching, the chair's comments on your research take much longer, focusing on how your research is measured in terms of its impact on the field, the level of the journals for your publications, and your ability to build upon and connect themes between your scholarly works.

As you leave your chair's office, you wonder, "Why isn't my teaching assessed with a similar concern for its impact on student learning?" While you are happy with receiving the "very good" classification for your merit review, in the back of your mind you are troubled that the discussion about a full year's worth of teaching lasted less than a minute. "Is that it? Does all the work I've put into my teaching—the countless hours of grading essays, my efforts to craft an intellectually coherent and systematically structured syllabus, my one-on-one interactions with students in and outside the classroom—all come down to being liked and having a good rapport with my students? And what about the evidence of my students' learning? Isn't it more important to consider how my classes build upon prerequisite materials and prepare students for graduation? Or to consider the fact that my students consistently score higher on common course examinations than those taking the same course taught by other faculty?"

Scenario Two: Department mailroom, where you encounter a colleague who has just come from teaching a class.

"Hi Christine, how was class?"
"I guess it was okay," she replies.
"Only okay?" you inquire.

Amazed that someone has an interest in her teaching, Christine unloads: "This semester has been tough. I'm not enjoying teaching this course. I just received their midterm projects, and after taking a quick glance at them, I honestly don't know if these students are learning what I thought they were. I'm beginning to wonder if my teaching is having any impact on them. I wish I had a way to figure out what's going on with this class, to really determine what my students are learning." As you briefly commiserate, you think, "Hmm. I had that same cohort of students last semester. I wonder if I prepared them well enough for her course expectations? How can we determine what students are learning over time?"

Scenario Three: Your office, where you are grading your students'
examinations.

As you are grading your students' midterm examination, you notice some common patterns in their answers. While your students
are doing well on the matching and multiple-choice questions,
their answers to the essay questions illustrate that they really don't
know the material as well as you would like. You begin to wonder
why they aren't able to tie concepts together to answer the essay
questions. For years you have stated in your syllabus that one of
your course goals is to build their critical thinking skills, but now
you wonder exactly what critical thinking means for this exam.
You begin to think about how you might restructure the homework assignments to address this issue. Then you wonder how
you might assess whether students can exhibit this higher-order
thinking in your classroom. But since your disciplinary area is not
educational research, you can't imagine how you would carry out
such an investigation.

Each of these three scenarios speaks to issues in making teaching and
learning visible, both to ourselves and to our colleagues. Even if you value and
support excellence in teaching, it is often difficult to capture the intellectual
work of your teaching in a form that can be conveyed easily to others. You
might be asking some of the following questions:

- How can I show the intellectual work of teaching that takes place inside
  and outside my classroom?

- How can I systematically investigate, analyze, and document my students'
  learning in relation to my teaching?

- How can I communicate this analysis and documentation of my teaching
  to campus or disciplinary audiences?

Whether you are a successful teacher who seeks to demonstrate the impact of your teaching more clearly, a beginning teacher who desires to improve your teaching of a particular course, or a teacher who wants to investigate a particular issue in your teaching, this book will be useful to you.

Making Teaching and Learning Visible: Course Portfolios and the Peer Review of Teaching is explicitly designed to help you conceptualize how your teaching, and the student learning that results, can be made visible. In particular, we offer a model that shows how you can draw upon a process of peer review to document, assess, reflect on, and improve your teaching and your students' learning through the use of a course portfolio.

The Intellectual Work of Teaching

There is much more to being an excellent and effective teacher than being a clear and engaging facilitator of class time with students. While time spent speaking or leading discussions in class is the most readily observable aspect of teaching, an instructor also does extraordinarily important work outside the classroom. Before the class even meets for the first time, for example, the instructor invests considerable time and expertise in the course design. He or she makes decisions about the goals of the course and identifies what successful completion means and looks like. The course goals might include knowledge and thinking skills, along with other characteristics such as interest in field, commitment to community, or awareness of cultural context. The course goals must be appropriate to the context—the program needs, institutional setting, and the students. These decisions require judgment and analysis, combining disciplinary understanding and a connection with colleagues and community. The teacher then designs a program of instruction that will maximize the likelihood of achieving the course goals; selects materials (books, articles, information from archives or other primary sources, online resources, and exhibits, or people outside the immediate school community); and develops learning activities (lectures, collaborative projects, discussions or debates, problem sets, writing). Since only one-third of students' time for a course is spent in class, the teacher takes great care to structure out-of-class work effectively.

Once the course is in progress, instructors need to carefully consider how well students are understanding the material. It is very challenging to develop opportunities for students to demonstrate that they have achieved the goals set out by the teacher. Constructing examinations, written assignments, and other opportunities for students to "perform" (i.e., demonstrate their understanding) takes time and skill. Having created an opportunity for assessment, the teacher draws on disciplinary knowledge to make explicit to the students the criteria to be used in evaluating those performances and to give students informative and helpful feedback on their performance.

After the course, an excellent teacher will also take the evidence of learning found in those performances and reflect upon what it says about the success of the course. It is intellectually challenging to identify the weaknesses in an instructional design and plan changes that might enhance the success of future students (and thereby of the teacher). In many cases, this involves making the results of one's teaching public and seeking comment from others, much as we do in other parts of our creative lives.

Our use of the phrase *intellectual work of teaching* is parallel to the notion of scholarly teaching that emerges from the work of Glassick, Huber, and Maeroff (1997). In their view, a teacher who acts in the manner of a scholar is well prepared, uses appropriate methods, gathers and considers relevant evidence, and reflects publicly on what has been learned in the process.

In a very real way, these aspects of good teaching are only partially visible to the students, or even to a colleague whose only contact with a course comes from visiting class sessions. Class visits can promote understanding of features of teaching such as clarity of communication or organization, respect for students, or enhancing interest in a field, and these characteristics also show up in student ratings of teachers. The intellectual work that underlies the class and that defines its success, however, can be seen through examination of course materials, student performances, and activities outside class time. Furthermore, that examination is best undertaken by someone who has advanced knowledge of the field being taught or rich experience in the practices of teaching in a similar setting. The fundamental purpose of the peer review of teaching is to provide occasions for just such examination of the intellectual work of teaching, including helpful and constructive feedback on that work from appropriate professional peers.

The Marriage of Peer Review and Teaching

Peer review involves having an individual with some measure of specialization or expertise provide substantive feedback on the quality of intellectual or creative work. We advocate peer review as a means to examine teaching because it holds a sacred place in academics—the opinion of peers is often viewed as the ultimate measure of quality and merit. Advocates of peer review assert that this process provides recognizable credibility to the materials being made public, such as a journal article that presents research findings. In addition to assuring quality, the process itself provides an opportunity to improve the work, as peer responders' reactions, comments, and suggestions are an invaluable guide for improved practice.

While peer review is routinely used in research, it is only gradually being recognized as a process valuable in the teaching arena, particularly in terms of evaluating teacher effectiveness. Until recently many institutions focused almost exclusively on student evaluations for measuring teacher effectiveness. These evaluations are useful for inquiring about what occurred during the time teachers and students spend together, but other aspects of the intellectual work of teaching are not always best reviewed by students. For instance, does a course have an acceptable level of academic rigor? Are objectives and topics appropriate to a course? Are evaluation methods fair? Does a course prepare students for advanced coursework? Does a course teach the needed skills to make a student successful in the workplace? These are the questions that your collegial peers—not your students—are qualified to answer about your intellectual work as a teacher.

Because of the limits of student course evaluations for evaluating the intellectual work of teaching, many schools also include peer judgments to evaluate teaching performance. A substantial body of research (e.g., Centra, 1993; Chism, 1999) describes various formats for peer evaluation of teaching, and much is known about how well these peer perceptions correspond with other indices of teaching performance. One of the most common approaches is peer observation, where a colleague or administrator observes a limited number of class sessions and writes a memo describing the instructor's ability to sustain students' attention in terms of coherence, clarity, and content.

It is our view, however, that *peer review of teaching* should refer to a much more complete examination of the intellectual work of teaching, and the term should be reserved for a process that goes well beyond the observation of a teacher's performance in the classroom.

While peer observation involves a colleague who presumably is better equipped than students to assess questions such as appropriateness of topics and objectives, it is still largely limited to the performance of the teacher during class time. Consider the following analogy. To assess your research capabilities, a senior faculty member in your department is going to observe you "doing research" for an hour. That is, he will watch you as you work at your computer, delve into an issue in the library, engage in dialogue with student assistants or research colleagues, or collect and analyze data in your laboratory. Based on his observation of how well you use your computer, how quickly you find books on the library shelf, or how efficiently the data are gathered in your laboratory, he will assess your skills as a researcher. You would probably agree that such a limited observation would be an incomplete assessment of your research productivity. At the very minimum, he would want to know how well you reflect on the evidence you gather and in what ways you report your conclusions to interested colleagues. In many cases, research is judged by the quality of the intellectual contribution made and how well the work is regarded by colleagues at other institutions. Having this same colleague assess the quality of your teaching by observing your classroom performance for an hour or two pales in comparison to the richness of his consideration of the real results of your research.

This is not to say that peer observation does not have a place. It does. Classroom visits can provide useful insight into your teaching practices and classroom mannerisms and offer some helpful feedback about how you interact with student learners. But this observation focuses primarily on your classroom presentation style and offers little information or evidence as to whether your students are learning and understanding the course material. To move beyond peer review focused solely on classroom observation, new models have emerged, models that take a more holistic approach toward capturing the intellectual work of teaching in all of its facets, both inside and outside the classroom.

Teachers who have been around universities for decades have seen many educational fads come and go, and they are generally not eager to try the latest fashion in teaching. When hearing about peer review, some veteran teachers may say, "You're just pushing the teaching practice du jour. You want me to teach like some imaginary ideal, but I don't need to. I lecture, they learn, that's all." Our model respects the diversity of teaching techniques and methods; we are not advocating a particular instructional practice. Rather, we are advocating *reflective practice*. You are asked only to reflect closely and carefully on how your instructional practices facilitate student learning regardless of the classroom approaches and techniques for achieving it. Teachers in large lecture courses, small discussion-based seminars, and online distance-delivery courses have all used our model. Our focus is on helping teachers document and make visible their teaching and their students' learning regardless of approach or technique. The only commitment this model requires of teachers is that they strive to maximize the depth and breadth of students' understanding.

The Course Portfolio as a Tool for Peer Review of Teaching

A *course portfolio* captures and makes visible the scholarly work of teaching by combining inquiry into the intellectual work of a course with an investigation of the quality of student understanding and performance. A course portfolio enables the teacher to document the careful, difficult, and intentional scholarly work of planning and teaching a course. It is also an invaluable tool for documenting and reflecting on the quantity and quality of student learning.

The concept of a course portfolio is not new. Certain disciplines, such as composition and studio art, have been very active in having students and teachers create reflective archives of their classroom work. Unlike a *teaching portfolio*, which typically archives essential course documents such as the syllabus, sample assignments, examinations, and evaluations, a course portfolio is a reflective investigation of how course structures, teaching techniques, and assessment strategies enhance or detract from student learning. As such, it provides a window into what occurred during the course, highlights what worked and what did not, and showcases the student learning that resulted. A course portfolio is an important departure from past practice since it allows a colleague or peer a deeper insight into a particular course.

In our model, peers participate in all stages of the course portfolio process. Internal peers from your department, college, or campus respond to your initial writing about your course and read and review the resulting course portfolio that you create. They then provide suggestions to improve your teaching as represented in your portfolio. In some cases, external peers from other schools read and assess your portfolio, either to help you develop your teaching or to evaluate your teaching. By sharing your teaching with many different peers, you receive helpful feedback that can strengthen your course design, teaching methods, and classroom assessments.

Course portfolios provide a foundation for generating ongoing professional conversations of the sort that you have about your disciplinary scholarship. Other potential uses of a portfolio include:

- Serving as a course repository and model to be used by future instructors

- Supporting teaching award applications

- Summarizing your teaching for annual merit review evaluations

- Documenting and assessing your faculty development efforts

- Highlighting your teaching as part of a promotion and tenure packet

- Structuring or showcasing a curricular revision

- Aiding in a department program review

- Supporting a job application

- Providing or assessing learning outcomes for department or program accreditation

- Serving as source material for a conference presentation or scholarly publication about your teaching

In addition to allowing teachers to reflect upon and analyze their teaching practices in a systematic and ongoing manner, course portfolios provide a mechanism for building interdisciplinary and interdepartmental campus communities that support and refine scholarly inquiry into improved student learning across programs and curricular areas. As a result, course portfolios have the potential to broaden the scope of these initiatives from individual classes to improving outcomes across programs, curricular areas, departments, and colleges.

The Value of Writing a Course Portfolio

For most teachers, starting to explore students' learning can be a bit daunting. You ask yourself some tough questions: Are my students truly learning what I think I am teaching them? Am I meeting my course goals? Are my course goals right for this course? Is the work that students do having any impact on their learning? Do the materials I have chosen build connections and perspective?

Where do you look for the answers to these questions? You might turn on your computer, collect all your course notes on your desk, and grab a stack of student papers that you have just finished grading. But you would probably find yourself wondering how to get started. Even though over the years you have given much thought to your course, this is probably the first time you have ever tried to create a written document that makes visible the intellectual effort you put into designing it and measuring its impact on student learning.

You are not alone. A professor of art and art history found herself in a similar predicament:

> I am a new teacher and an untenured faculty member. I teach intuitively. I go by how the class feels to me, and the overall atmosphere, and the general level of student response. I have a plan for each class day and I always vary it to respond to what arises in the studio. I used to feel strongly that the methods I used in a given situation were effective, but I never articulated why. I never voluntarily used the word "pedagogy" and was quite sure I never would. I was insecure about the intellectual underpinnings of my teaching and fearful I wouldn't be able to justify how I teach if necessary.

After developing a course portfolio, she wrote, "I found to my enormous relief that many of the methods I had chosen intuitively are used by other teachers and that they even have a pedagogical basis, which I am beginning to be able to articulate."

The course portfolio provides a framework within which you think about your course design, ask yourself if your classroom practices are working, and assess the level and range of student learning that goes on in your classroom. Unlike a teaching portfolio, which might summarize all the courses that you teach, a course portfolio is focused on a *single* course. More importantly, a course portfolio seeks to minimize the wheelbarrow effect of simply collecting all your homework, handouts, and examinations into one unexamined pile. Creating a portfolio for a single course can often be more valuable than a broad teaching portfolio since it is a concise and reflective document that can be shared with peers for their review of what student learning looks like in your particular course. For example, if you were to write portfolios on different courses, the insights that you gained in your analysis of each course could form the basis of the teaching statement that is the core of the more substantial teaching portfolio.

What constitutes a course portfolio is as individual as the instructor doing the teaching and the course being taught. Hutchings (1995) describes three common elements of a course portfolio: 1) explanation of the course design, 2) description of the enactment or implementation of the design, and 3) analysis of student learning resulting from the first two dimensions. Our model of a portfolio is similar and consists of the following essential parts:

- A reflective discussion of the content and goals of your course

- A description of your plans to accomplish key objectives in student learning

- Evidence, assessment, and evaluation of student achievement of these goals

- A reflective narrative on the relation among the above three elements

The raw material for the course portfolio is a set of three memos that you write about your course and that you then draw from to create a finished course portfolio that summarizes and analyzes student learning. The course portfolio emerges through the aggregation of the three memos about goals, methods, and learning. The faculty member's reflection on the relations among those elements is the connecting material that holds the portfolio together.

In this book we present models for two types of course portfolios: a *benchmark* course portfolio and an *inquiry* course portfolio. Each of these portfolio models offers a structure for exploring, reflecting on, and documenting a course. A benchmark portfolio presents a snapshot of your students' learning that occurs in one of your courses. This portfolio enables you to document your current teaching practices and to generate questions about your teaching that you would like to investigate further. An inquiry portfolio is useful for documenting improvement in teaching your course over time and for assessing the long-term impact of teaching changes, the success of teaching approaches, and the improvement in student learning. This inquiry process often moves teachers toward scholarship-of-teaching questions in their disciplines. In general, most instructors find it valuable to begin making their teaching visible through writing a benchmark portfolio. In subsequent offerings of the course, you might document the results of course changes with an inquiry portfolio.

You might be thinking, "Generate questions for further investigation? Document improvement over time? Looking at long-term impact of teaching changes? I don't want to become an educational researcher. I simply want to see if my students are learning what I think they are learning." This concern is common. But our model for course portfolios has been used by hundreds of teachers from numerous disciplines to provide a foundation on which to explore student learning. While these teachers had different teaching objectives and valued different forms of teaching, all of them found this process useful for thinking about their students' learning in a structured and systematic way. For example, a professor of English observes:

> Having a structure for reflecting on my course has been very useful for me. I have found that ordinarily after I finish a class I might have some thoughts about it—what happened and what I could do better in presenting the materials. Ideally after every semester I'd write these down, though in reality only occasionally have I ever taken the extra effort. The course portfolio framework has allowed me to think more systematically about my course and the activities that were happening in the classroom. Having to write about it and then share my writing with peers really forced me to look very closely at the things I was doing.

According to a professor of political science,

Writing a portfolio required me to be very conscious about how I was designing a syllabus, how I was evaluating students, and how I was approaching my teaching. It serves as a foundation on which my colleagues and I often start discussions about teaching and learning.

A professor of agronomy and horticulture emphasizes the variety of ways that a portfolio can be useful:

As I was describing the purpose and activities of the portfolio development progression to a colleague, I related that the process can serve many purposes, e.g., the creation of a course portfolio, documentation of teaching activities for promotion and tenure, a troubleshooting tool to assist in retooling an older or troubled course, but to me, it principally is a vehicle for an instructor to assess whether they are really teaching what they think they are teaching. I see it as more of a process than a product.

As these three teachers suggest, the process of creating a portfolio is often as valuable—or even more valuable—than the actual "product" generated in the end. While we agree that not all teachers need to be educational researchers, we do believe that if we want our students to be engaged in their learning, we ourselves need to be systematically and continually engaged in our teaching. Writing a course portfolio will help you become a better teacher, enhancing the classroom experience for current and future student learners not only in the course you are profiling but in all your courses.

The Portfolio in Context: History of Peer Review of Teaching and Course Portfolios

Our model of peer review is richly connected to the work of many others, and most of its structure and process derives from programs generated by other scholars of higher education. Putting the present examples in historical context may inform your own work on a portfolio and help you understand how the idea evolved in the American academic community. This background might also give you a better sense of why you would want to write a course portfolio or read one written by someone else. Efforts to "reform" how teaching is viewed and valued in postsecondary institutions have been driven by a collection of national initiatives by associations and foundations. For example, in 1987 the American Association for Higher Education (AAHE) sought to "address the need to improve America's schools and higher education" by making teaching at all levels "a truly respected profession." To carry out this work, AAHE asked three questions:

- Why don't university faculty see teaching as a subject worthy of discussion and study?

- Would teaching be improved if they did?

- What might be done to facilitate this shift in thinking?

In 1990, AAHE launched its Teaching Initiative to develop "cases" of teaching episodes designed to promote conversation about these questions. In that same year, Ernest Boyer published *Scholarship Reconsidered*, a report that sought to "reformulate the tired debate about teaching *versus* research" (Edgerton, Hutchings, & Quinlan, 1991, p. 1) by redefining faculty work as one of four forms of scholarship (teaching, discovery, integration, and application). Margaret Marshall (2004) describes the Boyer report as follows:

> an important exemplar of the rhetoric of reforming higher education that responded to the public criticism about undergraduate instruction and the poor quality of teaching in the nation's premier universities that arose in the 1980's and continued through the end of the century. (p. 66)

The publication of the Boyer report led to initiatives such as AAHE's Peer Review of Teaching Project and later the Carnegie Academy for the Scholarship of Teaching and Learning. These initiatives sought to document and reward postsecondary teaching in ways equivalent to traditional research activities. In other words, while the Boyer report outlined ways in which teaching could be understood as a scholarly activity, later efforts focused on how faculty could demonstrate the intellectual work that went into their teaching so that it could be better understood and rewarded within institutional structures.

Glassick et al.'s (1997) follow-up report, *Scholarship Assessed*, identifies six characteristics of the intellectual work done by scholars and explains how those characteristics can, in principle, be found in high-quality work in any of the four domains proposed by Boyer. Their analysis reveals that effective scholars have clear goals, make adequate preparation, use methods appropriate to their field of study, report results of their inquiry, reflect on the meaning of the evidence, and communicate clearly their conclusions. This elaboration of Boyer's ideas provides a conceptual framework that speaks compellingly to faculty who recognize these features in their own intellectual work, and that framework has been a very useful guide for considering how the peer review of teaching can be carried out.

The original peer review framework was developed for AAHE by Pat Hutchings, Lee Shulman, and Russell Edgerton (Hutchings, 1996), and it has been successfully used by faculty participants at dozens of institutions. In particular, Hutchings outlines three collaborative activities that highlight distinct features of teaching that can be simultaneously developed and evaluated. Participants exchange written memos on three topics, each of which becomes the subject of a subsequent conversation between the two teachers. The topics are 1) the content of a course, similar to an annotated syllabus; 2) the classroom practices, or more broadly instructional design for time in and out of class; and 3) examples of student learning, along with commentary on how well the work shown meets the instructor's goals for the learners. Hutchings' (1996) book on teaching as community property offers the foundation for the model that we present here. As an outgrowth of this AAHE initiative, Bill Cerbin (1994) created a course portfolio prototype for representing this thoughtful, intentional inquiry into student learning. This prototype has been formative for many teachers who have documented their work in publications such as *The Course Portfolio* (Hutchings, 1998) and *Opening Lines* (Hutchings, 2000). This work provided the initial blueprint for the prototype course portfolios that we used in our own campus efforts, and our colleagues have expanded on this original theme as they have written their individual works.

Our Model for Peer Review of Teaching

At the University of Nebraska–Lincoln, the use of course portfolios for peer review of teaching has developed and evolved over the past 10 years. Seven faculty members participated in the initial AAHE Peer Review of Teaching Project, and several dozen more completed a locally organized and federally funded series of summer seminars promoting peer collaboration in and review of teaching. With additional support from three foundations, this project has developed into a campus-wide, yearlong program in which faculty identify a course to examine systematically through the development of a course portfolio and in collaboration with colleagues. These course portfolios have proven to be a valuable tool for both teachers and readers in promoting reflection on successful teaching practices, encouraging conversations among teachers, and shifting attention to improved student learning. After the jump-start from external funding was over, the university continued support of the project with local funds; this stands as evidence of the value of the activity to the faculty. The fact that we, the authors, come from psychology, English, industrial engineering, and history is a clear indication that the model has value for capturing the intellectual work of teaching across academic disciplines. The program had the added benefit of building a community of portfolio authors who can participate as an audience and external peer reviewers for this new form of intellectual work.

The next goal was to refine and enhance our peer review model and extend it to other settings. Faculty members from Indiana University–Bloomington, the University of Michigan, Kansas State University, and Texas A&M University joined with Nebraska in a consortium to produce their own course portfolios, to support the development of peer collaboration on teaching, and to facilitate the peer review of those course portfolios. Since then, the Peer Review of Teaching Project has engaged hundreds of faculty members from these schools.

Early in the development of the consortium the project leaders developed a framework for a web-based electronic version of these portfolios, thereby providing potentially unlimited distribution for this newly elaborated intellectual format. The goal of this web site was to make teachers' course portfolios accessible for review and assessment beyond their local peers. As of 2006, more than 200 course portfolios are available for review by peers on the project web site (www.courseportfolio.org). A substantial number of these course portfolios are accessible to all readers, while others are part of the semipublic conversation about effective teaching within the faculty participants in the consortium. As a result of our campus and consortium efforts, we can testify to the value of peer review through course portfolios. This book will share ideas that we have borrowed from others, that we have developed and refined, and that we recommend with confidence as a solid starting point for any teacher interested in capturing the intellectual work entailed in teaching.

As one of our colleagues comments:

> I have always enjoyed the process of conceptualizing and designing a course, but through my yearlong participation in the portfolio process I have gained a much greater appreciation for the importance of carefully aligning course goals, instructional methods/materials, and activities/assignments to realizing student learning outcomes. In addition, I have gained renewed insight into the importance of making my expectations as explicit as possible, while still allowing space for students to approach their work creatively. More concretely, I also gained access to significant resources that will be useful to my professional development in the years to come. Through many animated discussions with colleagues I acquired new and creative ideas for instructional methods, assignments, and activities that I believe will support my course goals and student learning objectives. The various books on recent pedagogical developments that we received as participants in this process also were extremely useful in prompting meaningful reflection on this course. I appreciate the institutional reinforcement of the value of skillful teaching/learning and the support for my own professional development as a teacher.

An Invitation to Scholarly Teaching

This volume is offered as an invitation for three important audiences to learn about participation in peer review of teaching. We invite *faculty members* to participate with colleagues in scholarly consideration of your work as a teacher. We offer *faculty leaders and professionals* working in centers for teaching this practical guidebook that will help you introduce your colleagues to a process that has successfully enhanced teachers' enjoyment of scholarly teaching. We invite *academic and administrative leaders* to learn about the peer review of teaching and to consider this valuable process for your campus.

Throughout the book, you will find the first-person voices of teachers who have written course portfolios and colleagues who have reviewed the portfolios. The peer review of teaching can take many forms, and there is no requirement that you must engage in the full range of activities we describe. You can go as far along the path as you feel comfortable with or have time for, but we provide useful and practical guidelines for all phases of peer review of teaching. Likewise, you can pursue varying degrees of engagement with peers, from informal conversations to the regular exchange of portfolios. And your involvement may develop over time. For example, if you find informal exchange generative, you could then produce a reflective document that represents what you have learned from the exchange of materials. We have found that following the discipline of creating a brief written document generates richer insights and enhances what faculty learn from their interactions with peers. Just as the goal of scholarly research is to share what one has learned, likewise, the intellectual work of teaching should be shared with others in the profession. Exhibit 1.1 shows a continuum of engagement for peer review.

Exhibit 1.1 Continuum of Engagement

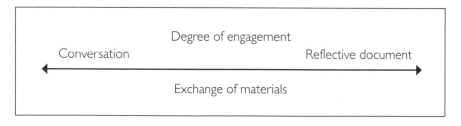

Degree of engagement

Conversation   Reflective document

Exchange of materials

Enlarging the Exchange

Similarly, there are varying degrees of public participation in peer review. It would be perfectly acceptable and valuable to engage only in the exchange of materials with a single colleague, offering and receiving comments on your ideas and practices. Many faculty members find this private exchange to be one of the most valuable parts of the process, and we provide a private space on our web site for these participants. Only when they are ready to have their work viewed by a larger audience do we move it to the more public space. In the long run, most participants are pleased to have their portfolios visible to all visitors to the Peer Review of Teaching Project web site. As with all other aspects of participation, the degree of public availability of a faculty member's work is determined by the author, not by the project leadership. Exhibit 1.2 shows a continuum of public access to the peer review work.

Exhibit 1.2 Range of Audience

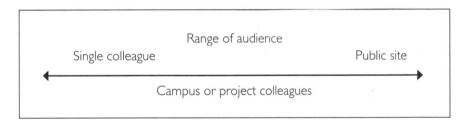

Using Peer Review of Teaching for Professional Growth and Advancement

In addition, you can choose how you use your materials and course portfolio once you have created them. It may be that you only have an interest in feedback for use in improving your students' learning; that would be how you would use your work. You could offer your portfolio for commentary from your local colleagues or make it part of a local conversation just as you might do with an early research result before you publish it. Should you feel your work represents intellectual work that you are proud of, you can also find an external audience to give critical review of what you have done and what your students have learned. As always, the choice of uses is entirely yours. The process helps you generate the representation of your work, and you choose the context for its uses. Exhibit 1.3 shows the range of options our participants have in using their course portfolios.

Exhibit 1.3 Range of Uses of Course Portfolios

It is important to note that this invitation does not require that you leave your role as a college teacher and become an educational researcher. Typically these portfolios are documents of informed and reflective practice, often including evidence from more than one offering of a course. They do not, however, generally include sophisticated additional measures or experimental designs that would allow in-depth consideration of theoretical issues in higher education. Indeed, we, the authors, come to this work as faculty members in several different disciplines, and most of the teachers with whom we work are not from educational research fields. We encourage teachers to draw upon their own disciplinary conventions of evidence and inquiry; the documentation and reflection on learning is best done using the lens of a specialist in the course content. As such, our peer review model provides a user-friendly way to represent inquiry into teaching and learning that is possible and even enjoyable within the boundaries of a typical faculty member's professional life. We are informed by the insights of our colleagues who engage in formal research in higher education, but we do not see this work as parallel to their scholarly inquiries. As such, it will not have the formal characteristics of educational research but will instead serve to provide benchmarks of the quality of teaching and learning that are taking place. Making those benchmarks public is a crucial first step in the establishment of communities that can promote excellence.

What's Next

We genuinely hope that this volume will make it easier for you to find the same joy of inquiry in your teaching that you already experience in other areas of your intellectual life. We have found that capturing individual teaching experiences through course portfolios and the peer review process builds powerful communities of engaged and excited teachers. To get you started in this intellectual activity, the remainder of this book includes detailed accounts of our peer review model and the work of many teachers who have generously made their teaching visible. The next three chapters detail the activities that yield the materials in a portfolio, complete with many examples. These chapters are a good place to start if you would like to generate a course portfolio to share with colleagues:

- Chapter 2 introduces the model for a benchmark course portfolio and describes the components for developing it.

- Chapter 3 provides examples taken from several different benchmark course portfolios to illustrate the process of writing a benchmark portfolio.

- Chapter 4 presents the second model, the inquiry portfolio, and illustrates the types of scholarly questions that teachers have investigated through this model.

The following three chapters address practical issues in sustaining the communities and getting external reviews when wanted, and they include the first-person voices of faculty participants describing their experience and its value to them:

- Chapter 5 explores the usefulness of external reviews in the peer review of teaching process and describes how to elicit and how to write a review of a course portfolio.

- Chapter 6 examines how the collaborative process of developing course portfolios influences the lives of individual faculty members and campus communities.

- Chapter 7 discusses practical issues in starting and sustaining a campus community of course portfolio authors and readers.

The final chapter will be of special interest to academic leaders and to faculty members who wonder whether this form of collaboration and interaction will be sustainable in American higher education. Thus Chapter 8 considers the current state of peer review of teaching, poses questions related to the scholarship of teaching and learning that teachers and administrators might consider as they integrate such processes within their school structures, and discusses the barriers to participation in peer review of teaching that should be considered in initiating a program.

Ultimately, this volume is designed to make it possible for you and others to join in this community of work around teaching, for purposes of both improving and evaluating it. You also might draw from our collective experience to create a parallel community of scholars with different emphases or purposes. The practices and examples presented here are not intended as standards or prescriptions for developing such a community. Rather, we encourage you to borrow and adapt these basic ideas to form your own vision of how to capture the intellectual work of your teaching in a way that can be represented, shared, reviewed, and celebrated with others.

2 Capturing the Intellectual Work of Teaching: The Benchmark Portfolio

A benchmark course portfolio presents a snapshot of student learning in your course and provides a clear record of your course design and teaching practices. Common elements of this portfolio include a discussion of your course goals, a summary of your classroom methods for achieving the goals, and evidence of student learning in meeting the course goals. This type of course portfolio offers a benchmark for documenting the student learning occurring in your course in a format that is available for sharing, use, and review by other teachers.

Start by Choosing a Target Course

To develop a benchmark portfolio, you need to pick a course that you want to profile. We call this your *target course*. This might be one you have taught many times before, or it might be a new course that you are designing. There are just as many reasons to target a course as there are courses to profile. A professor of advertising chose a course that she teaches every semester and that is required by the majors in her program:

> As a junior faculty member I am in the process of defining and fine-tuning all of the courses that I am teaching. My target course is at the heart of it all, because I teach it every semester and because it is one of the required courses in the advertising sequence.

I believe that writing this course portfolio will help me restructure the course and will provide a guide for other faculty who will teach it in the future or for the first time.

A professor of industrial engineering also chose her target course because she felt that it was in need of restructuring:

My target course is a junior-level statistics course taught to all engineering majors. A complicating factor with this course is that it is cross-listed with a similar course taught by the mathematics department. As such, the five different class sections taught each semester use the same textbook, cover the same course topics, and have a common final examination. I have taught this course nine previous times and I feel there are too many topics on the agenda for a single semester. Given the course is co-listed and there are multiple sections of it, it is not a simple process to change course topics. A focus of my portfolio is to explore the course and the resulting student learning to provide a foundation for my department to work with mathematics to redesign the ordering and coverage of course topics.

As these comments illustrate, creating a benchmark portfolio can be useful for encouraging conversations about teaching with colleagues, as well as for assessment and for curriculum development. The advertising professor is focused on developing a portfolio that can be used as a guide for other teachers, while the industrial engineering professor hopes to use the portfolio as evidence that a course should be redesigned. Other possible reasons for choosing your target course might include designing a new course that you have not taught before; examining a course you are not satisfied with, whether in terms of your own teaching methods or your students' learning; showcasing a course that you are proud of and that reveals your and your students' best efforts; or creating a course template that other teachers of the course can review and draw upon for their own teaching.

One important factor to keep in mind as you choose a target course is that the process will be most fruitful if you are not currently teaching that course but will be offering it in the very near future. It frequently happens that once teachers start exploring their target course, regardless of how many times they have taught it they want to make changes to the course design and to their assessment approaches. These changes are generally much easier to make before you start to teach that course rather than midway through a semester.

After you have chosen your target course, your next major task for a benchmark portfolio will be to write three different memos intended for a peer in your disciplinary area. As you write these three memos, you will reflect on your course syllabus and your learning goals for students, consider the particulars of your instructional practices, explain how your teaching methods are helping students meet the course goals, and document and analyze your students' learning. These memos have been modified from Hutchings' (1996) model of peer collaboration and review.

Benchmark Memo 1: Describe Your Course and Its Goals

What are the goals of your course? Who are your students? What do you want students coming out of your course to know or be able to do? You begin the process of writing a benchmark portfolio by writing a memo that describes your course, the goals, choices, and rationale that underlie the structure and planning of your course. One way to write the memo is to reflect on your course syllabus, whether it is one you have used before or one that you are now developing. Imagine that your audience for the memo is a peer in your discipline.

As you write about your course goals and objectives, you can also identify areas for revision or ways to articulate more clearly your teaching goals and plans. A professor (and department chair) of political science shares:

> Prior to this, I would ask, *What books do I want to use?* and then build my course design around those books. Oftentimes my book selection would reflect my own interest in what I wanted to read that semester. Now, when I sit down and think about my course, I begin with two questions: *What do I want to accomplish?* and, *What is it I want my students to know about polls, politics, and public opinions?*

When they are first asked to write this memo, many teachers initially react by saying, "I have been teaching this course for many years. I certainly know what my course goals are." But once they start to write the memo, and so articulate and clarify their goals, their view soon changes. For example, a professor of nutrition and dietetics realized that defining her goals for a course she had taught numerous times was complicated by a variety of voices identifying what students are expected to learn in her course:

> Some of these voices would include the university course cata-
> log, my department's expectations, our accrediting organization
> [American Dietetic Association], other colleges and departments
> which have approved this course as fulfilling a science require-
> ment as a non-lab science course for their majors, the textbook
> I have chosen, and comparable introduction to nutrition courses
> taught at other educational institutions. Adding to the confusion
> are my own personal goals for students in the course.

This teacher's experience highlights a similar issue you may need to re-solve: identifying and clarifying the external goals (What do others expect of students coming out of my course?) and your own internal goals (What do I want students to learn from my course?). Complicating the need to attend to multiple expectations of the course is your need to consider the direct and indirect learning goals for your course. Direct goals include what you want students to know or be able to do when they come out of your course. These goals are often the focus of assessment strategies. In comparison, indirect goals, such as developing critical thinking skills or making students aware of diversity and more involved with the world around them, are not as easily assessed. A professor of political science comments:

> The primary goal for my class is simple—to get students to think
> and, ideally, to care about international politics. In other words,
> I want to pull them in. I want them to leave this class wanting
> to read about and follow world events. In every class, I try to
> demonstrate how events in places like Bosnia and Rwanda affect
> them.

Once she had identified this goal, the challenge for this teacher was to create assessment strategies for ensuring she was meeting it. Similarly, by reflecting upon his course goals, a faculty member in construction management was better able to define and plan his course:

> The biggest impact on my teaching has been for me to refocus my thoughts concerning course development. Instead of developing presentation materials first and then creating assessments to see if the students mastered the issues, I now look towards the end of the course and focus on what it is that I want students to learn and then structure the presentations to achieve these goals. As such, instead of blindly hoping to achieve my course goals, I now aim directly at them.

Exhibit 2.1 provides prompts that may be useful in structuring Benchmark Memo 1. This first memo typically runs two to four pages. Teachers have told us that it generally takes approximately two to three hours to write this memo. These prompts are designed to help you to think about two issues: 1) how and why you teach your course as you do, and 2) what you want to accomplish through your course portfolio. (Chapter 3 provides examples of how different teachers have responded to these questions.)

Exhibit 2.1 Prompts for Writing Benchmark Memo 1

What is your course?

What is your course about? What is the content area covered? Who are your students (e.g., first year, second year, third year, fourth year, graduates, majors, or nonmajors)? What backgrounds do students bring to your course? How does your course fit into your departmental curriculum? Does it fit into curricula in other departments? How do your goals fit in with the goals of other courses in your department or discipline? Does your course lay the foundation for courses that follow it or build on what students have already learned in other courses? How is the course content connected to the general goals of your major or your college's general studies guidelines?

What are your goals for the course?

What do you want students to know? What do you want them to be able to do? What do you want them to understand? What do you want them to retain from your course? What perspectives or attitudes do you want them to have? What is important for them to learn about your field? What should they learn about themselves as students or as contributors to society? How are the goals structured into your course? Why is it necessary for your students to achieve these goals? What do you know about your students that makes these goals appropriate for their education? How are these goals reflected in the daily course structure and routines?

Why did you choose this particular course?

What is it about this particular course that led you to want to write a portfolio for it? Are there aspects of the course that you think are particularly noteworthy and that should be captured in the portfolio? Are there specific problems you face in this course that you would like to address in your portfolio?

Do you have any key goals that you want to acomplish by creating a course portfolio?

What aspects of student learning and of your teaching do you want to document and address by creating this portfolio? How do you foresee using your course portfolio (e.g., document your teaching, refine a course, disseminate to other colleagues, promotion and tenure)?

What sort of course portfolio would you like to create?

Will your resulting portfolio provide a broad overview of the entire course? Is it focusing on a particular aspect of the course (e.g., exams, assignments, projects)? Is your portfolio part of a larger departmental effort (e.g., curriculum development and analysis)?

Benchmark Memo 2: Describe the Course Activities

While you use the first memo to describe the goals for your course, in the second benchmark memo you discuss why you have chosen the teaching practices you use in the classroom and examine how these practices help your students to meet course goals. As such, this second memo helps you uncover and make visible the high degree of intellectual development and rationale that is embodied in the particulars of your course. For instance, if you are a history professor whose primary objective is for students to learn to think critically about the development of foreign policy, why and how do you use a particular practice, such as lecture or group work or a term paper, to help them achieve this objective? Similarly, if you are a biology professor, how does your structuring of the laboratory recitation sessions link to your goal of familiarizing students with biological systems? Your second memo asks you to think about these connections through writing about:

- The specific teaching methods, course materials, and course assignments you use to achieve your course goals (as described in Benchmark Memo 1)

- How particular aspects of the course (e.g., class activities, assignments, and other techniques) show evidence of and allow you to monitor and help direct student learning related to your course goals

As with the first memo, writing the second memo often helps teachers to see more clearly how they might want to revise their course activities. For example, as a result of exploring his classroom activities, a professor of computer science explains:

> I am more aware of things now. My delivery is less arbitrary and less regimental. I have always been able to incorporate games and fun stuff into my courses, but my delivery of regular lecture material was possibly a bit dull at times. These days, I think I am better at communicating and motivating the students about what I expect and what they should expect out of the course.

You might be thinking, "But I lecture to a large class and give multiple-choice examinations. I don't have the ability or time to teach this course differently." A professor of nutrition and dietetics faced a similar challenge:

> For quite a period of time I have struggled between my concerns for teaching in a large classroom [more than 200 students] in which lecture seemed to be the most efficient method of "delivering" what the students needed to know and knowing that there

were other, more effective, teaching strategies that did not include the good old standard lecture. I've also become increasingly frustrated with the use of technology as a teaching strategy. I have beautiful, colorful, PowerPoint slide sets for every single lecture of the semester. However, over the last year or so, I've noticed that I'm spending more time troubleshooting problems and quirks in using technology and less time on facilitating learning.

Our model for peer review and course portfolios does not advocate any specific teaching style or assessment strategy. As this teacher's example highlights, the key to this second memo is to document, reflect upon, and share your rationale, logic, and approaches for presenting and assessing the material and how these approaches are supporting your course goals. Once you have defined these approaches, you will use the next memo, Benchmark Memo 3, to focus on evidence that your students are learning what you want them to learn. Once that assessment is done, you will be able to confirm whether and to what extent your particular classroom approaches are supporting students' learning experiences.

As you write your second memo, you might find Exhibit 2.2 to be a useful guide. This reflective memo is typically three to four pages. You can write it prior to the start of the semester, or you can write it right after the course begins. Past experience has shown that it typically takes four hours to write Benchmark Memo 2.

Exhibit 2.2 Prompts for Writing Benchmark Memo 2

What teaching methods (e.g., lecture, group work, question/answer) are you using during your contact time with students?
How do you use each of these methods during class time and over the course of the semester? How does each of these teaching methods facilitate students' achievement of course goals? How do you measure student learning via these methods?

What course activities outside of class (e.g., projects, laboratory experience, Internet exercises, practica, or group work) are you using?
Why have you structured your activities in the way that you have? What, in particular, do you hope your students will learn from each activity? What are your expectations? How do you assess student performance at these activities?

What course materials (e.g., textbooks, course notes) are you using?
Why are these materials useful to students' achievement of the course objectives? How should students use each of the course materials?

What is the rationale for the methods you have chosen?
In what ways do you expect your choices for methods, materials, and assignments to assist your students in meeting the goals of your course? What influence has your discipline or field had on your choices? Why do you expect that the methods will be effective in promoting the learning you hope to achieve with these instructional practices?

How do your course choices link to the broader curriculum?
How do your choices of methods, materials, and activities build upon what students have learned in previous courses? How do your choices prepare your students for the broader university and/or department curriculum? How do your choices assist students in their future courses and/or endeavors beyond graduation?

Benchmark Memo 3: Document and Analyze Student Learning

In the first two memos, you wrote about your teaching as it is designed and proposed (through your syllabus) and conducted (through structured procedures and methods). But the conceptions and actions of teachers are only part of the educational picture. Effective teaching is also intrinsically tied to student learning.

We have all heard the familiar lament, "I'm an excellent teacher, but my students just didn't learn," or have had colleagues who boasted of their high teaching evaluation ratings but offered little evidence of their students' actual accomplishments. The third memo is intended to demonstrate the effectiveness of your teaching. It might be useful to think of the first two memos as an *argument* you are making about your course design and teaching practices and this third memo as the *evidence* or *data* that you are using to support this argument about your students' learning.

Exploring your students' learning in relationship to the course goals and your classroom practices is often an eye-opening experience for many teachers. A professor of special education and communication disorders comments:

> I chose my target course with the intention of trying to figure out what were the factors that made this class so miserable for me? Also, why was I so uncomfortable with this class? Why was I frustrated with my students? Writing this third memo forced me to look at all the data I had collected on my students' learning. I kept everything they did and then I made tables, matrices and graphs to answer lots of questions: How many students were distance students? How many were on campus? How many were majors? How many weren't? How many did well on the exam? How many didn't? Then I linked them by their demographic groups and began to realize that some of the demographics were factors and some of them weren't. Additionally, I was amazed and embarrassed to discover that I had course objectives I never taught, I had course objectives I taught but never assessed, I had course objectives I assessed and never taught, and I had material I taught and assessed but never listed as a course objective. By reorganizing the goals of my course, developing rubrics for evaluating student work, and assessing my classroom activities, I now have a focused approach for linking my teaching to my students' learning.

In the third memo, you provide evidence of your students' learning, understanding, or performance, and reflect upon their learning in relation to your overall teaching goals for the course. The foundation material for this memo consists of examples of your students' work. Unless, as we explore in Chapter 4, you are creating your course portfolio focused on a specific issue (e.g., the impact of a semester-long student project on student learning), it is best to collect samples of all relevant classroom work and activities so you have all of the available data to select from for your analysis.

From the collected student work, you can then choose one or more ways to document student performance. One method is to select *three* or *four* focused activities (e.g., homework assignments, examinations, projects) from your course that you would like to analyze with respect to student learning. In general, to keep this memo (and the resulting portfolio) small and useful, there is no need to showcase all the learning activities in your course. Highlighting only a limited number of the major course activities (e.g., a midterm exam, a term paper, a major homework assignment) will give a meaningful snapshot of what occurred in the course. Your overall objective is to have examples of the range of distribution for student learning through key classroom activities representing the class as a whole.

Because the activity of teaching varies widely across disciplines and contexts, there are as many different ways to document your students' learning as there are ways to teach. Exhibit 2.3 offers some collection strategies and presentation approaches for different types of classroom activities that you might wish to analyze. Which approach you decide to use will depend on the goal(s) for your course portfolio, the teaching activity, and the teaching questions you've chosen to study.

As an example, consider an economics professor whose assessment strategies include weekly quizzes, a midterm examination, two book reviews, a semester-long group project, and a final examination. Given the wide range of activities, how does she reduce her analysis to exploring only three or four specific activities? One approach would be to look at how the class points are distributed for each of the activities. In this example, the most points probably would be allocated for the midterm examination, the final examination, and the group project. Therefore, her portfolio could highlight the range of learning for each of these major activities. To do so, she would have to employ several approaches for collecting the student data. For the midterm and final examinations, her portfolio might highlight and reflect on examples of a high-, medium-, and low-performing student response to selected questions from each examination. In addition, she might incorporate a bar chart to highlight the distribution of class grades for each exam. To showcase the semester project, her portfolio could track the semester-long progress and growth of the same three student teams using their draft reports, final reports, and oral presentations to the class.

As you write this third memo, your goal is to reflect on how well your students have met the activity's objectives based on the evidence provided by

Exhibit 2.3 Collection Strategies for Different Classroom Activities

Collection Strategy	Type of Activity Useful For	Presentation Approach
Identify samples of student work that clearly represent high pass, medium pass, and low pass for a classroom activity	Homework assignment Quiz Book review Lab report Case study Oral reports	Present the range of student performance for the common classroom activity that occurs in your course. Then highlight a representative example of a low, medium, and high response to show your criteria for performance. For instance, suppose you give 10 quizzes over the course of the semester. Rather than present a detailed analysis for each quiz, share an overall assessment of how students performed on all 10 quizzes using statistics or a chart. Then select one quiz where students performed well and showcase a range of student responses to illustrate this performance. Next, select a quiz that the class overall did not do as well on. Reflect on why this might be and share a range of actual student answers.
Focus on students' responses to a small number of higher-order thinking questions for a classroom activity	Midterm examination Final examination	Rather than focusing on an entire examination, highlight and reflect on one or two questions out of the exam that differentiated student performance (perhaps focusing on questions where students had to exhibit higher-order thinking or synthesize several ideas or approaches). Reflect on what a high-, medium-, and low-pass student answer looks like. In addition, you could highlight the range of student scores (e.g., percentage of class to get a high/medium/low pass) for the question using statistics or a chart.

Collection Strategy	Type of Activity Useful For	Presentation Approach
Track selected students' performance on several assignments over the academic term	Student paper Research paper Studio project Writing assignment	Profile the growth and development of three or four students over the course of the semester. Highlight these students' work for two or three different projects. In addition, comment on how these students' performance reflects or illustrates the range of overall student performance in the class (how many achieved a high pass versus a low pass, etc.)
Follow selected students or student teams in their development of a single assignment over the academic term	Student project Group project Portfolio	Highlight the progression of student learning by focusing on the development of a single project or activity for three or four students or student teams. For example, an advertising professor might focus on how a handful of her students' portfolios develop and mature over the course of the academic term. In comparison, an engineering professor might showcase in stages how two or three student teams develop a project from initial conception to development of a prototype to presentation of a final report.

the student work that you have collected. For this reason, your memo should consist primarily of your interpretation of students' learning as demonstrated by their actual work. For instance, why did one student get an A and another get a C on a term paper? Why does one student's project demonstrate critical learning but another student's does not? How does a response to a certain multiple-choice question indicate that your students understood and mastered a concept?

This reflection on your students' learning often helps you identify and articulate the criteria that you may not have been aware of as you assessed and graded the student work. For instance, in having to write about why a term paper is a low or high pass, you may find yourself generating a set of criteria that you had not formalized when you initially graded the assignment. Teachers often find that writing about student performance in this way cycles back into their project assignments and enables them to articulate their objectives more clearly to students. For example, a professor of natural resources expresses a common outcome for many faculty as they engage in writing Benchmark Memo 3:

> I have added lectures, discussions, and activities that are directly tied to course objectives, and I better monitor student groups. In addition, I have created grading rubrics that force me to clarify my expectations—this has allowed my students to better understand what is expected of them.

Since Benchmark Memo 3 focuses on your reflection of student learning in your course, you usually cannot write it until the end of the semester during which you are teaching or immediately after. Instructors tell us that this memo is usually the most difficult and time-consuming to write. On average, this memo typically takes up to 10 hours. Unlike the first two memos, in which you write about issues that you as a teacher have considered when designing a course, analyzing and putting into context actual student work is a new challenge for most teachers and thus requires more time. Exhibit 2.4 offers prompts for writing Benchmark Memo 3. For each of the focused activities in which you will explore student learning, you should address the nature of student understanding and the distribution of performance. Once you complete this, you can reflect on overall student performance in the class.

Exhibit 2.4 Prompts for Writing Benchmark Memo 3

The nature of student understanding (for each focused activity you are analyzing)

1) Is there evidence (as represented in their work samples) of students meeting the specific learning goals you selected? Where do you see such understanding (cite actual passages from a student paper or a short answer from a quiz that provides evidence of such understanding)? What criteria did you use to assess this understanding?

2) How does the understanding represented by the work samples you present differ among students? How do these differences relate to the criteria you use in evaluating this work? How do these criteria relate to the intellectual goals you have set for the class?

3) Does performance represented by student work indicate students have developed an understanding for your field of study that will be retained and/or that students can apply to new contexts? In what ways?

4) What does your analysis of your students' work tell you about how students are learning ideas that are central to the course and to your teaching goals? Can you identify misconceptions they might have about these ideas? How might you identify and address these errors and/or misinterpretations?

Distribution of student performance (for each focused activity you are analyzing)

Given the evidence of student learning and performance that you documented above, what is the range or distribution for this learning activity within the class as a whole? In other words, how many students out of the total class population achieved a high, middle, or low range of success? How might you account for this range or distribution? Are you satisfied with this range or distribution? Why or why not? Does this range connect to your overall assumptions about the nature of student learning within this course? How might you represent this distribution of understanding to future readers of your course portfolio (e.g., via a graph or a pie chart)?

Student performance and the broader curriculum (for the overall course)

1) Overall, how well did student work meet your intellectual goals for the course? Did the distribution of student achievement meet your expectations? Why or why not?

2) Does the evidence of student performance you've documented above indicate that students are prepared for other courses or have achieved the aims of the broader curriculum? In what ways?

3) What does your students' work tell you about the prior preparation they have received in your area of study?

4) What changes could be made to help more students achieve in the higher categories of learning? Are there particular features of the course that you would redesign? What specific changes do you plan to make in the way you teach or organize the course the next time it is offered? How do you think those changes would improve student understanding?

Assembling the Course Portfolio

After you have written the three benchmark memos and have collected representative examples of student work, the final task is to link them together into a course portfolio that is accessible for use and review by fellow teachers. Some teachers develop course portfolios solely for their own formative use, but the majority of teachers write portfolios with peer readers in mind. They want the feedback a peer can provide.

There is no set format or checklist for developing a course portfolio since each is unique to the respective course, content material, course portfolio objective, and discipline. Because a course portfolio primarily represents your reflection on and analysis of your teaching experience and practice, you control the format and content of your portfolio. However, including specific key elements in a course portfolio can improve its accessibility and thus your reviewer's ability to respond with useful feedback. Exhibit 2.5 highlights the various components that you might incorporate into a benchmark course portfolio.

Most teachers scan representative student examples or extract a portion of the student work (such as paragraphs from a term paper) surrounded by teacher commentary and reflection as a way to include that work in their portfolios. Depending on the objective of your portfolio, other useful additions might include the following:

- A copy of your course syllabus

- Hyperlinks to a course web site(s)

- Inclusion of multimedia (photographs, video, audio) files

- Advice to others teaching a similar course and recommendations on teaching practices

- Course history and development (timeline, sequence, or stages); latest modifications (current web sites, new approaches, etc.); nature of modifications (teaching materials or methods, style or contents of tests) and rationale for revisions

You might be wondering if you should include your student course evaluations as part of your course portfolio. This depends on the objectives of your portfolio, but in general we would suggest that you do not include them. Your course portfolio is a supplement to the student voice in documenting the intellectual work and rationale for your course.

It is also important to remember that a course portfolio is not an archive of the course, but rather a *summary* of your own reflection on student learning and its relation to the course goals. As such, you should use reflection as a filter to decide what—and what not—to include. That is, the only materials (e.g., student examples, homework assignment descriptions, copies of examinations) that should be included with your portfolio are those upon which you *offer detailed reflection*. Correspondingly, a small excerpt of a course document or a student example is often better than including the entire item. For instance, there typically is no need to include a student's 30-page term paper in your portfolio. Rather, it would be better to extract several key paragraphs or sections from this paper that demonstrate why you consider it to be a high-pass, medium-pass, or low-pass example of student learning.

Because there are no formal formatting requirements for portfolios, their size can range from 15 pages to more than 100 pages. Length is driven by your ability to summarize your course and its impact on student learning as demonstrated through actual student work. When planning a course portfolio, remember that the purpose is to create a brief, reflective document that is readable by peers. In general, it is best to keep the narrative portion of your portfolio under 20 pages and to include supplementary material as an

Exhibit 2.5 Major Components of a Benchmark Course Portfolio

Section	Source	Topic
Introduction to the portfolio		A cover page with your name, department, course, university, and contact information
Table of contents		A listing of the sections in your course portfolio
Objectives for your course portfolio	Benchmark Memo I	• Your goals for writing the portfolio • Question(s) and issues you would like readers to address when reviewing the portfolio
Description of your course	Benchmark Memo I	• Description of your course and its context • A summary of course goals and learning objectives • Descriptions of the students in the course • Personal reflections on the chosen course • Place of the course within the broader department and university curricula
Teaching methods/course materials/course activities	Benchmark Memo 2	• Discussion of the teaching methods, course materials, and course activities used (e.g., lectures, labs, discussions) Mechanisms used to evaluate students (e.g., exams, exercises, quizzes, essays, problems, homework, attendance, participation) • Rationale for your teaching methods • Explanation of changed activities from previous years/sections

Section	Source	Topic
Analysis of student learning	Benchmark Memo 3	• Evidence and reflection of particular students and assignments on attainment of learning objectives (either incorporate examples in this discussion or have link(s) to student work in the appendix) • Overall analysis of final course grades and grade trends
Reflection on the course		• What you have learned in developing this portfolio • Future plans for the course (e.g., addressing misconceptions or problem areas) • Description of planned changes to the syllabus, delivery method, etc.
Appendixes		• A copy of the syllabus • Samples of student work not integrated into the main text discussion

appendix if necessary. Shorter portfolios are much better received than long ones and are therefore more useful. Potential readers of your portfolio, teaching peers, are as busy as you are and probably do not have the time or desire to live through a day-by-day description of your course. When in doubt, ask yourself, "Would I want to read this if my colleague gave it to me?"

Student Consent

Because the purpose of a course portfolio is to showcase and reflect on actual student work from your course, it is imperative to obtain your students' consent for collecting and then sharing that work. Early on in your course, you need to identify students who will consent to having their work potentially become part of your portfolio. Exhibit 2.6 is a sample student consent form that we distribute to and collect from students during the first week of class. (Chapter 8 includes a detailed discussion on the issue of student consent and institution review needed for collecting and analyzing student work.)

Exhibit 2.6 Sample Student Consent Form

The professor of this course is participating in an effort to develop new and better methods for promoting student learning. Your professor will be asked to evaluate his or her syllabus, exams, class activities, and written assignments. He or she will also receive feedback from other faculty members regarding teaching plans and how they are carried out. One of your teacher's goals is to improve student learning, and this cannot be accomplished without student input. Your professor will select several students whose work will be copied and included in a course portfolio to show how much and how deeply students are learning. This form requests your consent to allow your work to be considered for inclusion in your professor's course portfolio.

Please check the following designated purposes to which you give consent:

_____ I am willing to have copies of my coursework included in my professor's course portfolio.

_____ I do not want copies of my coursework included in my professor's course portfolio.

If you are willing to have your coursework included, check one of the following:

_____ I want my name to remain on any work that is used.

_____ I decline to have my name remain on any work that is used

Any additional restrictions on the use of classroom work (please specify):

Your name (please print) _____

Date _____

Phone number _____

Email address _____

Course title _____

Professor _____

By signing below you give your permission that work you produce for this course may be used with the restrictions and for the purposes indicated above. You understand that your grade is *not* connected in any way with your participation in this effort and that your anonymity will be maintained unless you designate otherwise. Finally, you understand that you are *free to withdraw consent at any time, now or in the future, without being penalized.*

Signature _____

If you have questions or concerns, please discuss them with your professor.

What's Next

This chapter has introduced you to the process of creating a benchmark portfolio. In the next chapter, you will see examples of actual teachers' benchmark portfolios along with their reflective comments on how writing their course portfolios benefited them as teachers.

3 THE BENCHMARK PORTFOLIO: FIVE EXAMPLES

This chapter describes in more detail the elements of the benchmark course portfolio introduced in Chapter 2 and provides examples from course portfolios written by faculty from five different disciplines. Stu Bernstein, who teaches in the construction systems department of the engineering college, wrote his portfolio for a class on construction planning and scheduling. Wendy Smooth, a political scientist, wrote her portfolio for her course on women and politics. Kathy Krone, a professor of communication studies, prepared her portfolio for a class on organizational communication. LeenKiat Soh, a computer scientist, presented his teaching from his "Introduction to Discrete Structures" course. Nancy Miller's portfolio highlighted her class on textiles and apparel merchandising.

We use these examples to show the components of a benchmark portfolio. As each of these portfolios illustrates, the three benchmark memos form the core of a benchmark portfolio. Your portfolio thus contains three elements: course goals, course activities, and student learning. First, you provide an overview of the course that moves from the broad and general, such as its place in your departmental or college curriculum, to the focused and specific, as reflected in your goals for the students taking that course. Then you describe the particulars of your teaching practice, ranging from course materials to types of assignments to specific teaching methods. Finally, you present evidence of student learning, along with your reflections on how well that evidence corresponds to and meets the goals you set for the students. You present these three elements within a larger context by including an introduction and conclusion that are tailored to your specific goals for writing the course portfolio, whether that is an explanation of those goals, a list of questions you would like readers to address as they review your portfolio, or a discussion of ways that you may change the course the next time you teach it. You can also use the introduction and conclusion as an opportunity to reflect on what you learned in the process of analyzing student learning and writing the portfolio.

You should write the first two parts of a course portfolio before you begin teaching the course; that is, while you are planning the course and writing the syllabus. Teachers tell us that the process of writing these two sections has led them to modify either their course goals or their instructional practices, which is much easier to do before the course begins than during the course of the semester or quarter. Once the course is over, you may need to update these sections to portray more accurately what actually happened in and outside of class while you were teaching, but you will seldom have to make major changes. The third part can only be completed after the course is over, but it also requires advance planning. Before the course begins, you will need to think carefully about the types of material you can use to document student learning, and as the semester or quarter progresses you must be sure to retain copies of student work that is returned to the students.

Let's look more closely at each step of writing a benchmark portfolio.

Using Benchmark Memo 1: Reflect on Your Syllabus

A course portfolio should open with a brief introduction to the course. Keep in mind that those who read your portfolio may be outside your department or even outside your institution, and many may be outside your discipline. In order to appreciate your pedagogical decisions, they must understand both the broader context and the circumstances under which you teach the course. Is the course required for majors, or is it taken by a broad range of students to fulfill your institution's general education requirement? Is it a large lecture course or a small graduate seminar? Is it part of a departmental sequence that either has a prerequisite or fulfills a prerequisite for other courses? The answers to these questions have a direct bearing both on your goals for student learning and on the methods you use to teach the course, and thus they should be made explicit at the beginning of your portfolio.

Describe the Course

A paragraph or two is usually sufficient to provide a description of the course, as demonstrated in Exhibit 3.1.

Exhibit 3.1 Kathy's Description of "Organizational Communication"

Description of the course

"Organizational Communication" is an upper-division course taken as an elective by communication studies majors and minors in the departments of advertising, biological sciences, broadcasting, management, psychology, and sociology. . . . This particular course is the only one our department offers that introduces undergraduate students to theories of organizational communication. While theoretical, the course also is practical in that it is rooted in the assumption that organizations of all stripes have the capacity to profoundly shape our communication and the quality of our lives. Because many of these processes are subtle, they often are poorly understood or taken for granted as "just the way things are." A course in organizational communication theory can raise students' awareness about many of these processes and cultivate the capacity to act more knowledgeably in organizations. To accomplish this, the course addresses traditional and contemporary modes of organizing and their implications for communication and quality of work life.

The course and the broader curriculum

Enrollment in this course is contingent upon having completed either Communication Studies 200 ("Introduction to Theories of Communication") or CS 201 ("Introduction to Research Methods in Communication Studies"). Students are not required, however, to have completed a lower-division course in organizational communication. This means students will have some background in general theories of communication or approaches to research, but they will have little to no background in organizational theory when they begin this course. . . . A course in organizational communication demonstrates how variability in organizational contexts both shapes and is shaped by these various communication processes. In addition, I developed this course with the understanding that it is one of the final courses that our majors will take before they graduate and enter the larger world of "paid work." The communication project and paper give them an opportunity to showcase what they have learned about effective communication in their previous courses and to strengthen their inner resources to better identify and cope with organizational communication dilemmas in constructive ways. Finally, "Organizational Communication" was approved as an integrative studies course that mandates the inclusion of significant writing and speaking components, as well as attention to diversity.

Explain the Course

Sometimes an instructor may want to discuss particular issues or challenges that teaching the course may present. In Exhibit 3.2, Wendy uses the description of "Women in Politics" to focus on students' attitudes toward the course and to give the rationale for her own teaching style. She also gives an overview of the course's structure and content.

Exhibit 3.2 Wendy's Description of "Women and Politics"

This upper-division political science course fulfills several different university requirements, such as the integrated studies requirements and other designations. Generally, it attracts around 40 students, but has had as many as 47 students enrolled. . . . A number of students have decided to major or minor in political science as a result of taking this course.

Meeting so many university requirements presents a series of challenges. The course attracts a diverse group of students from all over the university, and many of these students have very little knowledge of political institutions and are not familiar with the basic principles of political science as a discipline. In addition, political science students are not required to take this course. It is an elective for our majors, and many of them see it as an opportunity to explore this "media curiosity" of women and politics, yet they do not liken the course to other electives in the department that address political institutions, campaigns and elections, or the politics of particular regions of the world. I think that "Women and Politics" is largely viewed as a "fun" novelty course, which translates into a lightweight elective to balance out a tough selection of "real" political science courses. Students' expectations and motivations for taking this course are quite varied, and I have become more attuned to them, as they often present obstacles to meeting the goals of the course. Some students come to my course harboring resentment toward the integrated studies or diversity requirements and are resistant to the idea of a course like this one being required by the university above and beyond the courses of their discipline that "really matter." Others select the course because they imagine it as a simplistic discussion focused on the major political figures in national politics who happen to be women. Still others select this course because they entertain desires of one day becoming elected officials. This mixture of students with differing motivations and differing skill/knowledge levels dictates a certain balancing act between conducting the conversation at a level in which political science majors are stimulated and operating at a level that does not alienate students who are less familiar with politics and political institutions.

The situation is further complicated by my approach toward the study of women and politics. I study the spaces and social locations in which women typically experience politics—the realm of the familiar. As a result, much of the time in the course is spent focusing on and discussing the locations in which women engage in political action. I use this approach with an eye toward expanding the scope of what is considered "politics." Because we are studying the home, the family, the workplace, religious institutions, and social movements, students find themselves learning about subjects they did not expect to encounter in a women and politics course. It is not until the second half of the course that we start to study women in the institutions that they expected to study from the onset—the formal political institutions. The first section of the course lays the groundwork for understanding how and why women have entered the world of formal politics at the rates in which they have entered. It is also designed to help students understand that the formal institutions of politics are not the only locations of politics that are relevant to women's lives, and that women have been engaged in political activism in spaces that we do not traditionally regard as political.

In the second half of the course, we look at how women experience and engage in formal political institutions. By then, we have constructed an important framework for appreciating the advancements of women in formal politics. We focus on women as voters and as candidates for political office. We study the roles women play within formal political institutions and attempt to link the experiences of women outside of traditional politics to the roles they assume once elected to formal political institutions.

Discuss the Goals and Objective of the Course

Just as important as the course overview is a discussion of your goals and objectives for the course. Having to write about goals helps us to articulate or make visible the content knowledge, analytical or practical skills, and attitudes or outlooks that we want our students to have mastered or developed by the end of the course. In addition, verbalizing those goals often makes explicit the implicit assumptions about student learning that undergird all of our teaching. Discussing the goals for your course in your portfolio can therefore be a significant formative moment in your development as a teacher.

There is another very practical reason for making your goals clear as you begin work on your portfolio. If you can state your goals clearly and specifically at the beginning of your portfolio, you will find it easier to describe your teaching methods and assignments and to evaluate student learning. Walvoord and Anderson (1998) argue that effective grading begins with a clear conception of what teachers want their students to have learned at the end of the course. Specifying course goals, designing appropriate teaching and assessment measures, and analyzing student learning are all part of the same process. Your discussion of course goals will thus provide a framework for the rest of the course portfolio.

Whatever your goals and objectives for the course may be, you should not only state them but also explain your rationale for choosing them. This applies to your personal goals for student learning as well as to the more general goals for the course as part of your department or college's curriculum. If you list these goals in your course syllabus, you can simply refer to the syllabus (an appendix to your portfolio) and discuss the goals at greater length or describe additional goals that may not be clearly stated on the syllabus.

For example, after citing the course objective from the syllabus, LeenKiat explains more fully in his portfolio the motivational goals that are an important part of his course (Exhibit 3.3).

Exhibit 3.3 LeenKiat's Course Goals for "Introduction to Discrete Systems"

My syllabus provides the following statement of the goals for the course:

> The objective of this class is to familiarize students with some fun-
> damental issues in mathematics that are useful for problem solving
> and software design in computer programming. Essentially, this class
> aims at equipping students with powerful tools for their further
> study in computer science in general, and wonderful ideas for solv-
> ing programming problems in particular. Think about this: You will
> be able to formulate a problem in discrete mathematics that allows
> you to come up with a solution with confidence.

In general, I want the students to know that computer science is not just about programming, and that it is about how to solve problems better with a computer. There are many ways to solve problems, and one of them is to use elementary discrete mathematics. I want the students to realize the power and interesting applications of these supposedly boring and irrelevant mathematics to problems in computer science. I want them to be able to recognize a programming problem, find a solution, find a better solution (if there is one) using what they learn about discrete mathematics, and implement the solution. I want them to be able to look at a problem from different perspectives, not ad hoc but formulative, not satisfying but optimizing, not guessing but knowing that the solution will work, and so on. I want them to understand that discrete mathematics is not some far-fetched, out-of-reach jumble of topics that have nothing to do with computer science. I want them to understand that discrete mathematics is fun when you start to think about how useful they can be and start to solve problems using these relics. I want the students to retain from my course that mathematics is important in computer science, as it opens up a whole branch of possible and sometimes better solutions, and all the topics that are covered in the course. I want the students to have a positive attitude towards this course, at least towards the end of the course. I want them to feel this course is worth their trouble. I want them to understand why computer science departments all over the country stick this thorn in their curricula.

The goals are structured into my course through my handouts, my lec-tures, and my assignments. I give out about a dozen handouts, called "Light-bulbs," to students on each topic covered. Each Lightbulb is a document of five to six real-world problems, observations, or applications that are related to the topic in question. With these, I put the students into the context and I am able to convince them of the importance of this course, thus *motivating them to not distance themselves from this course....* My second goal is *to instill a problem-solving, inquisitive mindset in my students.* My third goal is *to make them realize that hard work is required to do well in anything, and to achieve what they set out to do.* These are three of my overall goals for all my courses. I want to *inspire* them.

As for this particular course of this exercise, these are some additional goals. First, I want the students *to learn really well the basics of discrete mathematics,* not the "how," but the "why" as well—e.g., why logic is useful, how we can apply it to real-world problems. Second, I want the students *to be able to relate what they learned here to other disciplines.* One thing that I emphasized in the class was that as long as you understand the motivations behind the ideas, then you would know how to use those ideas. The technical details are often forgotten after the class but the key, fundamental ideas should stay with the students forever. The strategies used in solving problems, the analytical behavior, and so on, are important. I want the students to learn these reasoning tricks, to become empowered by logic, and be able to argue and present their own ideas with mathematical or scientific confidence. Third, I also want the students *to understand the materials intuitively.* I want them to realize that these seemingly "untouchable," "sophisticated" subjects are actually part of our common sense. Once a concept is understood, that should stay with the students forever. And I want to encourage them to relate those concepts to other problems, to their interests.

Some of your course goals may be imposed from the outside, whether by your department as a whole or by an accrediting agency in your discipline, but there is almost always room for you to incorporate your own concerns and emphases. For instance, Stu's years of experience in the construction industry shape the goals for his course on construction planning and scheduling, which emphasizes the real-world application of managing a construction project (Exhibit 3.4).

Exhibit 3.4 Stu's Course Goals for "Construction Planning and Scheduling"

Proper planning and scheduling is more than just a task to be accomplished on the job, it is a mindset. To instill this thinking in the students, I encourage them, from day one, to use this thought process in their daily lives. All students have personal and academic lives, and most have professional ones, as well, all of which need to be properly planned and then scheduled.

One goal of this course was for the students to be able to *define all of the activities, that are the components of a project.* In order for them to be able to do this, they needed to use the lessons taught to them in previous classes. These included drawing interpretation, business methods, and estimating. One of the first things they learned to create, in order to accomplish this goal, was the *work plan.* This is a written summary of how they plan to accomplish their project goals. One of the many things I taught the students was to be able to logically deduce the relationships between activities, i.e., the sequence of the project. They needed to be able to put themselves on the job site (in their mind's eye) and decide how they wanted to construct the project, and what were the logical sequences to accomplish this, keeping in mind cost, time, and quality. This led to one of the next goals, which is *the ability to create a work breakdown structure.* The work breakdown structure is a list of project activities, which are organized in groups, subgroups, etc. It is a tool that encourages the person to organize the activities into logical sections. This exercise is helpful as an aid in thinking through the project and determining the activities necessary to complete the project.

Once the students were comfortable with the reasons for properly planning and scheduling not only construction projects, but activities in their personal and academic lives, it was time to provide them with the basic tools, while stressing the importance of using them properly. These tools included resource leveling, resource allocation, and precedence diagramming. One of the goals that I stressed strongly in this class was that *the students should leave this class to become project managers and not babysitters.* I encouraged them to take charge and control their projects, not sit back and record what occurred on them. I stressed that the training they were receiving would enable them to anticipate the problems and challenges that may occur on their projects, and instill in them the desire to be proactive instead of reactive. So, another of the course goals was to *motivate them to excel in their craft.* To begin this process, I tried to motivate them to excel in school, thereby creating a mindset that mediocrity is not acceptable. . . .

Another very important goal of the class was *reinforcing communication skills, particularly the ability to make presentations.* The construction industry is getting away from "hard bid" projects and moving toward negotiated work. The firms that are hiring our students are looking for people with the ability to sell themselves, their company, and their projects. To this end, I assigned two major presentations, and I took every opportunity available to get the students to feel comfortable speaking in front of others.

Another goal was to *introduce the use of computer scheduling software.* While I believe it is more important for the students to understand the principles of planning and scheduling, it is still important for them to be able to navigate their way around popular industry software. Therefore, I introduced the use of scheduling software as a secondary function to having the knowledge necessary to create the input. Prior to introducing the scheduling software, I showed the students a number of ways they could use a spreadsheet program to accomplish many of the same functions on their own.

The ability to productively function in a team setting was another important goal for this class. There are very few roles in the construction process that allow a person to work solo on a project. At some point or another, they are going to be part of a team, or group, with a common goal. The ability to work on a team is fundamental in this course, in this curriculum, and ultimately in their careers.

Explain Your Design for the Course

In structuring both her course and her course portfolio, Nancy found it helpful to follow the principles of backward design described by Wiggins and Mc-Tighe (2001). They suggest that a teacher begin by identifying desired results, then determine what would be acceptable evidence of having obtained those results, and finally plan specific learning experiences and instruction that will bring about the desired results. In her portfolio, Nancy outlines the goals for her case study approach (Exhibit 3.5).

Exhibit 3.5 Nancy's Application of Backward Design in Developing Her Merchandising Course

Teaching methods: Rationale for adopting backward design, problem-based learning, and case studies

The problem-based learning experiences in this course are located at the heart of the discipline, in that students shifted from the role of a knowledge receiver to the more active role as a constructor of meaning. . . . Students became aware that each situation holds unique aspects requiring diagnoses and understanding prior to judgment and recommendation. . . . The pedagogy of the case method of instruction is predicated on the benefits of acquiring practical experiences by means of simulated reality with problem-based exercises.

Application of backward design in developing the merchandising course

Stage 1: Determination of desired enduring outcomes (general, major objectives): Upon successful completion of this merchandising course students will:

1) Perceive current and predict future economic, political, and social trends and their implications for the textile and apparel industry

2) Acquire a realistic understanding of historic and contemporary opportunities and challenges confronted by consumers, and by big and small-sized retailers and producers within the textiles and apparel industry, including social responsibilities and ethical practices within the industry

Stage 2: Determination of acceptable evidence
Students must perform several tasks in addressing each case situation, which serve as evidence of their understanding. First, they must assume the role of the individual in the scenario and react as they believe that person should. Second, they should justify their course of action from among the alternatives available. Third, they must make written and verbal recommendations based on facts concerned with the case, concepts, and principles from class notes, and outside sources such as readings and guest speakers, or from current economic, social, or political affairs. Fourth, it is a given that there will not be enough information to solve the problem; however, students will employ common sense and logic, as actual business owners and managers realistically do, in formulating the plan of action. Fifth, during class discussion of solutions, students should be willing to submit their conclusions to others for examination, and expect as well as tolerate challenges to the views expressed. Sixth, in discussions with others, students should be alert to new insights provided that may result in revisions to the analysis and recommendations.

Stage 3: Determination of learning experiences and instruction
After developing a comprehensive list of concepts considered essential for effective leadership in the field of merchandising, I created several course-related activities in and outside of class. I wrote five new case studies, each focusing on the crucial knowledge and skills students need to demonstrate their understanding. Simultaneously, I established a rubric for evaluating the performance tasks and evidence of understanding for each case. . . . Following development of the case studies, I wrote lectures supporting the case situations and collected resource materials from Internet sites, federal agencies, and assorted current

readings and made them available for student use.... I selected guest speakers for their specific area of expertise relative to each case study. In addition to case studies, I based the course grade on four short quizzes and participation in class discussions. Students evaluated themselves and others on their case study teams. Students gave ongoing feedback throughout the semester regarding the ability of the guest speakers, the lectures, the readings, and the instructor to facilitate their achievement of objectives, in addition to the formal UNL [University of Nebraska–Lincoln] evaluation at the end of the course.

Nancy's example demonstrates the close relationship between her course goals and her instructional practices. The second component of your portfolio will focus more specifically on those instructional practices—the textbooks, assessment measures, and use of classroom time—that you use to help your students learn.

Using Benchmark Memo 2: Explain Instructional Practices

To illustrate your teaching and assessment methods, you may include examples of assignments, projects, and exams as an appendix to your portfolio, but this section of your course portfolio should be more than simply a collection of handouts. Just as important are your reflections on your use of those handouts: Why did you choose a particular form of assignment or design a project the way you did? The answers to these questions give readers a better understanding of your teaching than they would get from simply reading through the assignments. For example, LeenKiat's two paragraphs describing his "Lightbulbs" reveal more about his pedagogical methods than the 30 total pages of handouts could do, but LeenKiat also gives the URL for the web site where those readers who would like to see the handouts can find them (Exhibit 3.6).

Exhibit 3.6 LeenKiat's Description of His Teaching Methods and Course Materials

Teaching methods
The class is almost entirely lecture-based with the usual questions and answers

interwoven, supplemented by handouts, "Lightbulbs," homework assignments, and so on.

I have to cover a certain number of topics in the semester, and so I have to cover these topics quickly. However, one thing that I always emphasize is problem solving. I always try to put the topics being covered in the context of real-world problem solving, linking the disparate topics together in one single theme. I transition between one topic and the next by reviewing what we have done and what we are going to do, and why we are doing it.

I give handouts in the class to supplement the textbook. Note that these handouts are not my lecture notes. They are summaries, or key principles or ideas, or tables, or rules that I have collected from other textbooks. I organize them into more readable and understandable form for the students. I give out about 20 handouts in the class. I use these throughout the semester. I think these handouts reinforce what the students learn in the class with my lectures. I do not measure student learning via this method. However, from the response of the students, I get a sense of whether a handout is well received.

I also discuss Lightbulbs in class. I post 10 Lightbulb documents on the class web site. I go through each Lightbulb in class as examples to link the subjects with some real-world examples or applications. For example, I use the Chevy Chase *National Lampoon* story for Hamilton and Euler circuits, and Monty Python's *Holy Grail* for a discussion in predicate logic. There are other examples as well. My goal here is to try to let the students know the following: "Even though the forms you see, the letters you see, the symbols you see in the textbook, on the board, in the homework assignments, may look strange and nothing like the world you face, these are very useful, powerful ideas that you have been using, and you will be using in the future for your problem solving, in the industry, in academia, in sports, at home, in any setting."

I give lectures throughout each period. Each lecture involves a tutorial discussion, followed by a set of examples on the board, working through each example step by step, allowing the students to think and reflect on what I do. I try to make my lectures interesting, with a lot of passion and enthusiasm, to rouse interest in the students.

I give pop quizzes to force students to attend recitations. I use these to measure how prepared the students are with the materials. Based on these, I give more examples in my lectures to clarify their confusions. I think these quizzes force the students to study more often and ask more questions.

This time around, I experimented with the "ask the neighbor" idea that I learned from a conference that I had just attended. I give each student a piece of paper to write down a question on a particular topic that I select. After five minutes, the student hands the paper to another student to rate from 1 to 10 in terms of difficulty. This rating process is repeated two more times to other students. In the end, I ask the class to hand me questions rated with 27, 28, 29, or 30 points and solve these questions in class. Before the class ends, I collect all questions. After the class, I review and re-rate these questions and give them out as handouts with my rating and the students' rating. That way, I know what the students expect to be difficult questions, and the students get a sense of what I think are fair questions. Moreover, this exercise also challenges the students to come up with good questions—and that is a powerful learning approach. Furthermore, this exercise provides the students with many practice questions. Finally, the students really enjoy this.

In addition to describing his course materials and use of classroom time, LeenKiat explains his requirement that students go through their exams individually with him (Exhibit 3.7). Simply including a copy of the exams without any further explanation or reflection would not have revealed this significant opportunity for students to receive feedback on their performance. The exam alone would not fully reflect his teaching practices.

Exhibit 3.7 LeenKiat's Description of Course Activities

Course activities

I give three examinations (including a final). After each examination, I always ask the students to pick up their exams individually; they must see me in my office before getting their exams back. I spend time with each student individually, ranging between 15 minutes and 45 minutes per student. (Yes, this is really time-consuming, especially in a large class like mine.) I go through each exam question, giving feedback, asking the student to explain better. . . . After going through the exam, I encourage the student to be more diligent, more motivated, more open, and visit my office hours more often. I emphasize the importance of knowing the taught subjects, and so on. I am sincere in my interviews, trying to make the students understand that I will help them as long as they help themselves and show initiative to want to do well, and giving them tips and guidelines on how to do things better. So, in a way, I try to motivate them and also show them specific methods on how to study better.

I give 11 homework assignments, including programming ones. This is the main staple of my reinforcement for the students. Each homework assignment is quite "heavy duty," and is scheduled about 10 days apart. Thus, the students get to work on a lot of homework assignments. I think this allows them to study and to work hard. I measure student learning by grading some of the homework assignments myself and re-addressing questions that have been troublesome.

I maintain a class web site where I post the solutions to my quizzes, homework, and exams. Students read them.

Rationale for teaching methods

Since this course typically involves a large class size, I choose teaching methods that will allow me to interact with the students in class time effectively and efficiently. Group-based discussions or activities are not feasible as it is not straightforward to break the class up into groups. Thus, I use lecture-based delivery. I do not use any slide-based presentations as I prefer going through each example carefully, putting myself in the shoes of the students, thinking out loud all the necessary steps and decisions that I make when I solve a problem on the board. I ask a lot of questions in class and encourage show-of-hands responses from the students. I also give the students a lot of handouts, summarizing key points in each subject. I aim to improve their self-efficacy in understanding the subject topics.

Further, I prefer incorporating real-world problem solving into my course materials and my teaching as well. For example, I use the "ask the neighbor" method to some degree of success. Examples and problems that I give are often based on real-world problems. I often use examples in engineering, business, software, physics, biology, and the arts. Here, my rationale is to improve their motivation in learning the subject topics.

Discussion of teaching practices and assessment measures is also important for highlighting types of learning through methods other than the traditional lecture. Classroom observers in Kathy's course on organizational communication would note her use of PowerPoint and videos to enrich her lectures, but they would not see her contact with students through her use of Blackboard (course management software) or their collaboration on group projects outside the classroom. Note in Exhibit 3.8 that after describing her course materials and use of course time, Kathy places the rationale for her teaching practices in the larger context of the pedagogical approach characteristic of communication studies.

Exhibit 3.8 Kathy's Course Materials and Goals

Course materials and methods

In introducing the required reading and materials for the course, I discussed the importance of maintaining a dynamic interplay between the received knowledge students would be acquiring from outer voices of authority (i.e., researchers) and the inner knowledge they are developing based on their own experiences with organizational communication. The required reading included a widely adopted organizational communication textbook, a supplemental trade paperback that illustrates stresses and strains of the 21st-century workplace, and five case studies. I also required students to read several web sites illustrating the communication practices of highly progressive organizations, as well as ones illustrating the darker side of organizational communication (e.g., workplace bullying). I relied on current events such as the space shuttle Columbia and Challenger explosions to illustrate the systems and cultural approaches to organizations and ways in which these approaches go beyond more traditional approaches to help illuminate faulty decision-making within NASA and the space shuttle program. I also used a variety of video excerpts and in-class exercises to illustrate formal knowledge about organizational communication. The textbook is very useful in familiarizing students with foundational knowledge of organizational communication studies. The other materials were intended to bring to life many of the theories and concepts introduced in the textbook.

I also incorporate the use of PowerPoint and Blackboard in this course— PowerPoint to illustrate key concepts/ideas, and Blackboard to maintain contact with students to remind them of deadlines and assignments. With PowerPoint, I am attempting to incorporate more visual images in my slides in an effort to illustrate concepts more holistically and to reduce the amount of written text on each slide. I was interested in learning whether such visual representations of theoretical ideas facilitate student learning. Through my participation in the portfolio process I also became acquainted with a "lingering questions" exercise that I used to collect student feedback following our unit on critical theory and organizational communication. The theoretical language of this particular approach is highly abstract and unconventional, which might discourage students from applying it to understand organizational communication problems. Through this exercise I was able to gain more insight into those concepts that students found particularly difficult. This feedback will be very useful as I continue revising lectures and exercises with an eye toward making material more accessible and meaningful to students.

I believe this array of materials and methods is effective in structuring sufficient opportunities to develop the capacity to analyze organizational communication challenges in a more theoretically sophisticated way. The methods I use are very much in line with those used in the wider discipline of communication studies. Demonstrating relationships between theory and practice is a hallmark feature of the pedagogy of communication studies. Cultivating the capacity to become more reflective about communication behavior and to turn to theory to guide personal and professional communication choices, are key features of undergraduate instruction in communication studies.

Outside course activities

I used case studies to provide students with opportunities to understand and address consequential organizational communication problems from a variety of theoretical perspectives. Cases and questions were distributed in advance and students were instructed to familiarize themselves with each and to sketch out the contours of their responses to questions prior to coming to class. Questions invited them to apply theoretical concepts to understanding the problems in the case and to suggesting ways of addressing each problem. Students completed five of these one- to two-page, in-class writing assignments throughout the semester. Each was followed by small group discussion of their responses and then discussion among the larger group. The total of students' scores on each of these papers constituted one-half of their grade for class participation. Students also collaborated on a group communication project and paper that required them to locate a local organization, identify one of its communication challenges and design a project that would help the organization meet that specific challenge. In the process of completing the project, students were required to draw upon course content in developing a description of the organization, its day-to-day internal and external communication practices, and the types of communication challenges it faced. The quality of work on this assignment was evaluated according to the extent to which the project helped the organization meet one of its communication challenges and the skillfulness with which students applied course concepts in their description of the organization, its internal and external communication practices, and the types of communication challenges it faces.

The complement of teaching is learning. Thus the description of and reflection on your instructional practices should be followed by an analysis and interpretation of the learning that occurs in your class over the course of the semester.

Using Benchmark Memo 3: Document and Analyze Student Learning

Many people find that documenting and reflecting on student learning is the most difficult part of writing a course portfolio. It can also be the most rewarding, because it stimulates our personal development as teachers. Reflecting on and articulating what our students have learned often causes us to reconsider and redefine course goals, to modify existing teaching practices, and to experiment with new ones. In Exhibit 3.9, Nancy describes how her evaluation of student learning caused her to refine her teaching through the course of the semester and has given her ideas for how to improve the course in the future.

Exhibit 3.9 Nancy's Integration of Feedback From Her Evaluation of Student Learning

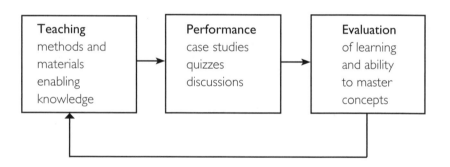

The cyclical nature of constant evaluation throughout the semester allowed me to refine and adjust the course content and measures of learning. Prior teaching of this course was more linear in that the course was established allowing only a small degree of flexibility throughout the semester. . . . In addition, evaluating the students at the end of their program of study has allowed me to see what is needed earlier in their program and that can be addressed in my reformulation of a sophomore-level course. I have found this experience to be very beneficial in organizing, developing, and explaining the course in its new format.

Document Student Learning

To document student learning, you must collect examples of student work and other information from the beginning of the semester or quarter that may be useful for determining the extent and nature of student learning at the end of the course. Like any research activity, it is far easier to write this portion of the portfolio if you have a broad range of material to choose from. You will need to be selective, though, in determining how you document student learning. A good rule of thumb is that you will only include a specific example of student work in your portfolio if you explicitly discuss how that example displays what the student has learned. As with your discussion of teaching practices and assessment measures, your analysis of student learning should focus on how your examples reflect student learning, and the relevant portion of the students' work can be included in an appendix.

The type of information that you use to document student learning can vary considerably, depending on both the nature of the course and your particular goals. For example, some teachers collect all the work done by a small group of students throughout the semester to show improvement in those students' learning. In Exhibit 3.10, LeenKiat's discussion of how three different students performed on their exams illustrates how student work can be used to evaluate changes in content knowledge and practical skills, as well as intangible areas such as fostering motivation and inquisitiveness.

Exhibit 3.10 LeenKiat's Analysis of Student Learning

Analysis of student learning: The nature of student understanding

I have three intellectual goals in teaching this course: 1) to motivate students to not distance themselves from this course; 2) to instill a problem-solving, inquisitive mindset; and 3) to make them realize that in any endeavor, hard work is required to do well and to achieve what they set out to do. As for goals for the students, I want the students 1) to learn really well the basics of discrete mathematics, 2) to be able to relate what they learn here to other disciplines, and 3) to understand the materials intuitively. Here I present the work examples of three students in the three examinations (exam 1, exam 2, and final): students A, B, and C [the three examinations and their solutions are included in an appendix to the portfolio].

Student A's exam 1, exam 2, and final

- In exam 1, student A scored a 57%. Looking at exam 1, you will see that student A was able to do problem 2, receiving full credit for that. For problem 1, student A made a mistake in part (i). A minor mistake in terms of using a "union" symbol instead of an "intersection" symbol was, however, a key conceptual mistake. It was not a careless mistake: he failed to translate "the set of customers who bought a reference book and a children's book" into "the intersection between two sets." In other words, he failed to grasp that particular topic of sets and failed to apply it. In problem 3(b), student A showed again that he failed to transfer what he learned to a less familiar problem setup. This problem was actually a reduced version of an example given in class. However, the students were not given many homework questions in this topic. Thus, apparently student A was not familiar with this topic and, from his "2, 4; substitution" response to step 5 in this problem 3(b), I could tell that he was throwing darts a little bit. Finally, in problem 4, student A was not able to work on most of the four subparts. He was only able to provide a little bit of solution for 4(a). However, from the little piece of this solution, I concluded that he actually did not have a clear idea of proofs in prepositional logic. His solution, though short and incomplete, had a big mistake that showed lack of understanding.

- In exam 2, student A scored a 98%. He did extremely well. From his handwriting, I could also see that he paid more attention to his solution, showing all steps. Thus, I think I have succeeded to some extent in motivating my students to work hard. His solution to problem 4 showed me that he really understood the materials. The steps were logical, well thought out, and methodical.

- In the final, student A scored a 93%. He did very well. His change in this class observed in exam 2 carried through to this exam. His solution to problem 4 (a prepositional logic proof) showed me that he understood the materials very well. This problem is of the same topic that he failed so miserably in exam 1. So, it was good to see that he was able to conquer the topics in which he had not done well.

Student B's exam 1, exam 2, and final

- In exam 1, student B scored a 69%. Looking at exam 1, we see that student B was not a careful student. He made some obvious mistakes or skipped some key steps. For problem 4, he was able to solve one subpart correctly, and started on the other two subparts with no mistakes. However, he ran out of time and did not finish most of problem 4. I thought student B was good enough to do very well in this class—only if he was more careful and had more time.

- In exam 2, student B, however, scored a surprisingly low 68%. Once again, he made careless mistakes and skipped some key steps. It was a pity. Looking at how he was trying to solve problem 4, I had no doubt that he understood most of combinatorics. However, he did not seem to be careful and willing to pay attention to his work. As a result, his grades suffered. This is a student who could have done much better had he paid more attention to his work. The way he failed problem 2 was a telltale sign of a student who had not a clue about proof by induction.

- In the final, student B scored 72%. By this time, I kind of figured out that the student was definitely capable of doing well in the class yet was not motivated to study and prepare for the examinations. He did well in the problem-solving type problems (4 and 6). But he performed poorly in the new topics: trees and graphs, especially for problem 3 on trees. This was a problem on which most students received full credit. However, student B lost 19 out of 25 points on this particular problem. So, his carelessness and non-attentiveness hurt him.

Student C's exam 1, exam 2, and final

- In exam 1, student C scored a 99.5%. He did an excellent job. His solutions were methodical, logical, efficient, and elegant. He showed clear understanding of the proofs, tackling them with ease (few changes in his solution), and with a clear focus in each.

- In exam 2, student C scored a 95%. Once again, he gave complete, clear, efficient solutions. He stumbled in problem 4, missing parts (a) and (d) quite seriously. However, even when his recognition of the problem was incorrect, his solution showed me a great deal of understanding of the subject matter.

- In the final, Student C scored an 89%. I believe that he was careless this time around, or at least, did not go through the final as carefully as he should have. He lost 9 points on his induction problem (5), the same type of problem that he received full credit for in exam 2. He made two key, uncharacteristic mistakes.

Regrettably, I was not able to secure the examinations of one particular student, "John Doe." His first two examinations' scores were 60% and 61%, respectively. I took extra time discussing with the student on the topics before the final for 3–4 hours. We went through a handful of examples. And the student did very well in the final: 85%!!! This is wonderful to see. And this time around, his work showed that he had learned well about the concepts . . . his work showed understanding and logic, and consistency! I am very happy for this student's effort.

Evidence of students meeting the specific learning goals?

Based on the above three sets of examples, I see evidence that students are meeting the specific learning goals. Those like student A worked harder and received a higher grade in the second examination. That satisfies my "working hard" goal. Those like student C showed that they had a clear understanding and grasp of the subject matter. However, those like student B showed no motivation as they did relatively poorly in their second examination while other students did so much better. Even when they failed to receive full credit for some problems, those like students A and C were able to show me their problem-solving strategies—sound and logical. And I rewarded them accordingly. For exam 1, I use problems 1 and 4 as the criteria to assess student understanding. For exam 2, I use problems 2, 3, and 4 as the criteria to assess student understanding. These problems are "application"-type problems.

Understanding represented by the work samples?

The different levels of understanding are reflected in the work samples collected for the students. Student C, a student with clear understanding of the basics of discrete mathematics and of the basics of problem solving, provided very clean, focused, efficient solutions. Even when he failed to solve a problem, he was able to provide logical strategies demonstrating a good grasp of the subject matter. Student A, who fared poorly in exam 1, was able to turn around and did very well in exam 2. In exam 1, even though he couldn't finish some key problems (ran out of time), he failed to understand logical proof, for example. In exam 2, even though he seemed to have enough time to do everything, he demonstrated superb understanding by elegantly solving problem 4. Thus, if we took out the time issue, there is clear evidence that student A improved so much from exam 1 to exam 2 in terms of his understanding of the subject matter. That is very encouraging. Finally, student B, who scored similarly in both examinations, continued with his trend of carelessness and lack of attention. He did have glimpses of brilliance in him, solving some difficult problems well, but failing miserably in some knowledge/memory recall type problems.

Discuss Different Levels of Student Achievement

Another approach is to select examples of student work on the same assignment that demonstrate different levels of learning, such as high pass, medium pass, and low pass. This method allows you to give a holistic glimpse of all students' learning in the course by presenting a representative sample of the various levels of performance. It is particularly effective if you state what proportion of students were distributed at each level of learning and can demonstrate that a significant number either performed consistently at the higher levels or moved from a lower to a higher level over the course of the semester.

You do not need to include the entire assignment in order make these differences clear. As Exhibit 3.11 shows, Kathy explains her criteria for differentiating between these levels and then gives excerpts from three different examples of a case analysis that illustrate these differences.

Exhibit 3.11 Kathy's Analysis of Student Learning

Case analyses

In completing a series of five case analyses, students practiced applying a range of theoretical ideas to understanding and addressing a variety of communication dilemmas. Their work on these assignments promoted the development of judgment concerning the advantages and disadvantages of various approaches to organizing, the types of communication challenges produced by each, and the ways each would go about addressing those problems. To document and analyze student learning via case analyses I selected samples that represent high-pass, medium-pass, and low-pass work.

High-pass work consisted of selecting a higher number of theoretical ideas (10–12), accurately describing each, and providing convincing examples of how each idea is illustrated in the case. Medium-pass work consisted of selecting a slightly fewer number of concepts (7–9), and providing less convincing descriptions and examples of each. Low-pass work consisted of selecting still fewer ideas (4–6), and providing less convincing descriptions and examples of each. In the first assignment, students were asked to analyze the problems emerging when a small, locally owned ice cream shop called Creamy Creations was sold to a large, national fast-food chain. The new owners proceeded to streamline and standardize operations in order to increase efficiency and sales. Students were asked to analyze the potential problems in light of classical approaches to organization including Frederick Taylor's theory of scientific management and Max Weber's theory of bureaucracy.

Following are excerpts from <u>high-pass</u> work on the initial assignment:

- *Jennifer: The premise that there is only one best way to do a job is clearly illustrated. The Burger Barn eliminated the traditional operational style of the business in order to implement the style they felt was best for efficiency and profit—despite the feelings of customers and employees. They felt there was only one best way to run the business. Scientific management theory calls for the proper selection of employees, but the Burger Barn essentially ignored this premise. They felt any unskilled worker could do the job, so turnover was high. Strict division of labor also applies to this case. Management made decisions that the employees followed. Centralization of power is another component exercised. The Burger Barn makes all decisions for Creamy Creations whether it be how the business is run, line operation or future expansion. In addition, the shop becomes a closed system. Opinions of customers who preferred the previous atmosphere—a local hangout—are not taken into consideration.*

Following are excerpts from an example of <u>medium-pass</u> work on the initial assignment:

- *Teresa: Authority was definitely taken [sic] with the Burger Barn managers. They delegated the work assignments to the employees. The employees didn't have much say in them. Also, discipline was being used. I assume that some of the employees didn't like how Burger Barn was running the business.*

Following are excerpts from an example of <u>low-pass</u> work on the initial assignment:

- *Joan: The bureaucracy management [sic] is exactly what went in to effect when Burger Barn took over. There were fixed division of labor rules. They divided their stations into three main purposes: scooping, topping, and paying. The personalized creation was more like an assembly line at this time.*

In reflecting on student learning related to this assignment I learned to be more explicit about the number of concepts necessary to earn high, medium and low scores. I also learned to be more explicit about the importance of concept selection, clear description, and accurate application. I became more keenly aware of how students with well-developed writing abilities are advantaged by this type of assignment. Making my expectations more explicit gave those who were less-gifted writers additional support for their efforts. In reflecting across student performance on the entire set of five assignments, I noticed that the greatest improvements in student performance occurred from time one to time two. Performance then tended to level off or even drop back down after a one-time improvement. Such a pattern indicates that individual motivation plays an important role in sustaining a high level of student performance across a series of assignments such as this.

Include a Variety of Student Work

Demonstrations of student learning do not need to be restricted only to graded work. Kathy found it useful to give her students a pre-test during the first week of class that served as a baseline against which she measured their performance on a post-test given during the last week. The post-test showed that students had become more sophisticated in their thinking about organizational communication as a result of the course, a finding that supplements the results of the graded assignments for the course (Exhibit 3.12).

Exhibit 3.12 Kathy's Pre- and Post-Tests

Pre- and post-test descriptions of effective organizational communication
The purpose of this exercise was to assess change in students' thinking about organizational communication effectiveness as a result of their participation in this course. I was hoping that students' thoughts on organizational communication effectiveness would be more complex and finely nuanced at the end of the semester than they were at the beginning. To gain insight into any changes that might have occurred, I asked each student to explain what he or she thought were the best ways to organize and communicate during the first week of the semester, and then again during the last week of the semester. Both were ungraded written exercises designed to provide broad feedback on student learning that could be useful in my ongoing efforts to continue developing the course.

One change that occurred reflected increased complexity in how students thought about organizational communication, with one commenting that "'organized' seemed like a very simple word before I had this class" and another indicating that his understanding of organizational communication had become "deeper and wider." More specifically, many students reported now recognizing that there is more than one way to organize and communicate in organizations. As one student said, "I've learned so much about how to manage and organize … the only way to know the best way is to know why all the other ways don't work or have their individual problems." Along the same lines, another student commented, "I have learned that there really is no 'best' way. … The only best way is to look at your specific situation and people involved and adjust to that." And this sophisticated change in learning came from an academically gifted student who said, "I think that integrating the approaches to organizing is the best strategy. Organization can be achieved on a variety of levels via a vast array of methods. Choosing the best method for a particular situation is important. Having many options to choose from only enhances the probability of embarking upon a successful organizing task. The only way to learn such strategies is by studying the various methods—as we did in class."

Other students commented on their newly acquired understanding of the relationship between organizational structures and communication, and of organizations as communication systems and cultures. I was very pleased to see that one student learned that effective "communication in an organization is more than treating others nicely. It involves groups and systems." Another student explained, "I learned that how one communicates may depend on the structure and expectations of that organization," while another indicated, "I still believe that the best way to communicate is treating people the way you want to be treated," but that "in this class we had the opportunity to look at certain hierarchical control methods and how they can either inhibit or promote care and respect for employees."

In describing the best ways to organize and communicate, several students moved beyond the contingency approach represented in the students' remarks above and went so far as to take a stand in favor of more participatory, less hierarchical forms of organization. This group of students was able to note a greater recognition of the communication problems associated with traditional, hierarchical forms of organizing and a newly acquired appreciation for the benefits of collaborative, team-based organizing. As one student put it, "Before I said a clear leader was the best way, but now I think the team-based organization achieves just as good results … each member must feel their opinion counts in order to be satisfied with decision making." Another student was able to see that while she first thought that breaking things down into parts was the most effective way to organize, she now could see "how the creation of [such] differences leads to separation in the organization that must be overcome through communication." Still another student wrote, "I thought hierarchical separation of power was the best way to organize, and now I think team-based management is the ideal situation; team-based management puts different departments together causing them to work together," while another student wisely commented that "when communication is widespread, understanding throughout the organization is evenly distributed."

Clearly, there is some evidence to suggest that students' thinking about organizational communication became more contingent, more complex, less unconventional and more novel by the end of the semester.

Beyond individual performance, Kathy also describes and analyzes the performance of her students on the group project assignment (Exhibit 3.13). Her reflections have stimulated her to think about ways to improve the course, in this case by making her assignment description more explicit.

Exhibit 3.13 Kathy's Analysis of Group Project Work

Communication project and paper

The purpose of this assignment was to provide students the opportunity to practice applying their knowledge of organizational communication to understanding a specific organization, its communication challenges and helping to address one of these. Working in small groups, students identified a local, nonprofit organization that was willing to collaborate with them on this project. Students were required to interview a representative from the organization to learn more about its structure, its internal and external communication and the communication challenges it faced. Working with the organization, they selected one specific communication challenge that their work on this project would help meet. The paper reported on the organization's structure, communication and challenges and discussed how their communication project helped meet the specific challenge. Prior to the project/paper deadline, I distributed a checklist for students to use in making sure their projects/papers contained the required elements. Papers/projects were evaluated according to how well the students evidenced knowledge and understanding of organizational communication theory in their description of the organization, its communication challenges and in the development of their projects. The quality of group work on the project and paper ranged from very high pass to lower pass. In this section, I reflect on those qualities that produced two very high-pass papers/projects, and one high-pass paper/project.

The groups of students who constructed two of the very high-pass projects/papers managed to identify a specific communication challenge, construct a useful project that could make a difference, and also to write about the organization and their project in ways that reflected a broad and deep understanding of organizational communication concepts/theories. In reflecting further on these two papers, however, I also am remembering that both groups sought my feedback. One group sought feedback throughout the entire process, while the other group submitted a draft of their paper for my review two weeks in advance of the due date. Both groups were very open to my feedback and able to incorporate it into their projects/papers. This most likely contributed to their earning very high scores on this assignment and also helped me clarify my expectations for students on this assignment. I plan on revising the assignment sheet so as to be more explicit about my expectations.

The group of students that constructed the high-pass paper/project created a project that had the potential to make a significant difference in how the organization met one of its communication challenges (e.g., "Parent Sportsmanship Agreement"). However, the group's description of the organization, its internal and external communication, and the nature of its communication challenges drew exclusively upon a narrow range of concepts from classical theories of organization. Because this was a local organization, dependent almost entirely on volunteers, ideas from classical theory could not capture much of its unique character. So, while the group developed a communication project that was quite useful to the organization, their paper did not demonstrate the ways in which this volunteer organization depends on "self-organizing" for instance, or on how the larger culture of fan incivility at sporting events possibly contributes to the misbehavior of fans at the local Lincoln Little Chiefs baseball games. In reflecting upon why this might have occurred, I have wondered about the tendency for students to select the earliest and most obvious approach to organizations, and about the wording on the assignment sheet asking students to describe the organization's structure. This language is more consistent with the traditional approaches to organization and does not make clear the fact that the contemporary approaches might be able to better explain an organization such as this. Only the top student papers drew upon language from the systems or cultural approach in analyzing the organization and constructing their communication projects. While student motivation and ability play some role in their performance on this assignment, I also can see the need to make the assignment sheet more explicit in inviting students to draw upon a range of theoretical approaches, or even to specify that they draw upon at least two or three approaches in their analysis of the organization.

Reflect on Student Work

As these examples show, reflection on student work often helps us to see where we can introduce changes to help our students learn. Exhibit 3.14 reveals how Wendy's analysis of her students' response papers helped her see not only differences between students, but also common problems that gave her ideas about how to improve this particular assignment the next time she teaches her course.

Exhibit 3.14 Wendy's Analysis of Student Learning

For the remainder of the course portfolio, I am reviewing the student discussion-leading projects by analyzing students' response papers. I chose to analyze the students' response papers during the week in which they presented for several reasons. The students tended to prepare more when they were presenting and they tended to put more effort toward their readings and their papers. With this paper they also tend to put forth a more concerted effort to link their responses to the larger themes of the course. Reviewing this response paper also allows me to analyze how they are working within their groups.

Across the board, I learned that students need more direction in writing their response papers. Students were instructed to offer a reaction to the readings rather than summarizing the readings. In offering a reaction, students could discuss how the readings are related to one another in a given week, how the readings relate to other themes we have discussed in class, the relevancy of the readings to some current political event or to raise critical questions about the author's approach to the topic. I used the response paper assignment as an opportunity to have a one to one discussion with students regarding their thoughts about the readings. Given that not every student is going to talk in class, the response papers offered an opportunity for students to illustrate their critical thoughts on the readings. Students were required to submit their first response paper early in the semester to receive feedback before moving to the next paper.

The most common problem that students encountered in their reaction papers was the tendency to summarize the readings rather than analyzing the readings [portfolio has a hyperlink to student example I]. Instead of offering his own ideas about the readings, this student's paper amounted to a general summary of the articles. In comparing this response paper to others submitted by this same student, I also suspect that this response paper was the one the student put the least amount of effort into as opposed to other papers in which he did engage in the level of critical thinking that was expected for the response papers. The next time I teach the course, I will offer more directions and even examples of strong response papers so that students are more clear about what I expect in the response papers. While summarizing was clearly a problem for students, some students were able to move beyond summarizing and raised critical questions regarding the content of the material [portfolio has a hyperlink to example II]. This student raised questions regarding his previous conceptualizations regarding the issue of representation by elected officials. He uses the readings as a springboard to examine his own preconceived notions regarding the ability of those outside of a certain group to adequately represent the needs of another group. In raising these questions, he focuses on specific passages from the text to support his points. This paper received a high grade given its attention to detail, its reflective nature, and integration of the week's readings. The student also shows a level of deliberation over the readings and raises critical questions regarding the findings of the authors.

Some students used the response papers to make connections to their life experiences while also making connections to the themes of the course [portfolio has a hyperlink to student example III]. This student focuses on her own personal experiences with a woman advocating for the rights of a disabled child. In disclosing this personal experience, the student relates this experience to the women in the readings who became activists as a result of the need to represent the interests of their children. Some students use their response papers only to discuss their personal experiences with little relation to the readings and these papers are evaluated lower, because I am interested in students tying their personal experiences to the readings for the course. This student is able to relate her own experiences to the readings and meets one of the course goals by discussing her responsibility for changing how she personally views the issue. The student also reflects on her responsibility to participate in society, changing its perspective, which reflects the course goal of instilling a responsibility for social change in students. The student also demonstrates an understanding of many of the broad goals of the semester and offers some reflection over her accumulated learning across the semester. She discusses her challenges in using various lenses to analyze the world and demonstrates that she is trying to understand others' perspectives that differ from her own. She also makes linkages between our earlier class discussions on women of color's activism despite limited resources to the reading she is currently doing on the experiences of women parenting disabled children. She is able to articulate the connections between the two groups of women using limited resources to achieve challenging goals.

In this response paper, students were also asked to reflect on the group process and to evaluate their fellow group members. Unlike the final project, in which they are required to complete a quantitative evaluation of their group members, students are only expected to assess the group's work in the final paragraph of their response paper. This did not yield what I expected. Students were not reflective of how the group process worked or even critical of their colleagues' performances. Instead, they most commonly used this time to describe how the work was divided among the group members [portfolio has a hyperlink to student example IV]. The last paragraph of this student's paper is typical of how students approached the evaluative portion of the assignment. The next time I make this assignment, I will provide specific questions for students to assess their colleagues' performances. Since students did not use this opportunity to be reflective on the group process, I designed a questionnaire at the end of the semester that required students to reflect on how they learned this semester.

Use Quantitative Analysis

Quantitative analysis of student learning, such as an analysis of grade distribution for individual exams or final grades, can also be revealing. Just as with your qualitative analysis of student work, however, any presentation of course statistics should include your interpretation of and reflection on those statistics. LeenKiat's analysis of grade distribution on each of his course's three exams led him to conclude that the higher grades on the second examination were not due solely to his having made the exam easier than the first exam; rather they also reflected an improvement in student learning (Exhibit 3.15).

Exhibit 3.15 LeenKiat's Quantitative Analysis of Student Learning

Distribution of student performance

I am using my exams as the documented evidence of student learning. The figure below shows the grade distributions for exam 1 and exam 2. In general, students did much better in exam 2 than they did in exam 1. The number of students who did very well (in the grade A range) jumps from below 20% to greater than 35%. Upon closer analysis, this was due to some B students in exam 1 doing better and promoting themselves to the A range. Quite a few of C students in exam 2 also moved up in grade range to B. Table 3 shows the average gain and drop in terms of exam scores.

Grade distributions for exam 1, exam 2, and final

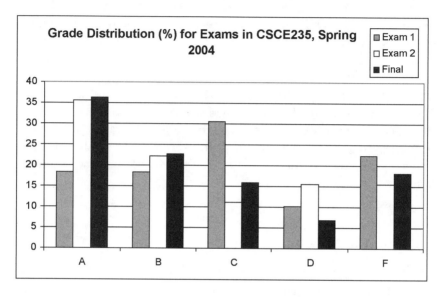

Note. Grade A is 90 and above; grade B is between 80 and 89; grade C is between 70 and 79; grade D is between 60 and 69; grade F is 59 and below.

The following table shows the specific statistics of the three exams. In terms of average, exam 1's average was 72.8%, exam 2's was 78.6%, and exam 3's was 77.5%. I am happy with that. However, if we look at the median, the students did much better in the final (87%) than in exam 2 (85.0%) and in exam 1 (75.5%). . . . The final was comprehensive and students had been trained quite well after making mistakes in the first two examinations. . . . The fact that many students did very well, in the A and B ranges for exam 2, concerns me.

Specific statistics about the three examinations

Statistics	Exam 1	Exam 2	Final
Number of students taking exams	49	45	44
Average	72.8%	78.6%	77.5%
Median	75.5%	85.0%	87.0%
Low	34.0%	16.0%	6.7%
High	99.5%	98.0%	100.0%
Standard deviation	16.51	17.65	21.30

Now, let me rehash a little. This is the third time I have taught this class. In my first two classes, I had a significantly different group of students. When I teach, I interact with my students a lot; at least I try to pose questions to them, go through examples with them on the board, trying to get them to interact with me. In the first two classes, the students were not responsive. Almost never did the students raise their hands when I asked, "Who thinks this is correct? Please raise your hand." But with my current class, I immediately noticed a difference: these students responded to my prompting. It was very encouraging to see. The class was more lively and exciting. So, going into exam 1, I expected the students to do well, at least to perform better than the previous two classes. The accompanying figure shows the averages.

Average scores for exam 1 and exam 2 for the three CSCE235 classes that I have taught

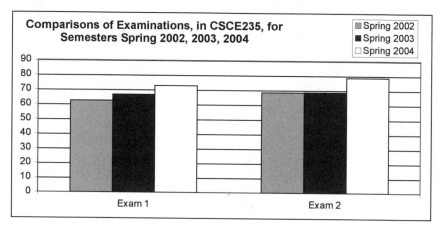

I draw two key observations from this figure.

- First, for exam 1, the scores matched my expectations and my impression about this class. The students did better. Actually, by putting them together this way, I realized that the scores for exam 1 have gradually improved at about 6% over these three classes, while the difficulty level and number of questions in the examinations have been very similar (but the questions themselves, of course, are very different).

- Second, for exam 2, I realize that I might have overcompensated. This is due to some quite vocal protests after exam 1. Students complained about not having enough time to finish the examination. At first, this puzzled me. These students performed much better than the students in the past, yet they complained about not having enough time, while the students in the past never did that. Actually, the students in the past almost always finished their examinations on time. This time around, when I called time, only a few students handed in their exam 1. The others were still scribbling away! After the initial puzzlement, it dawned on me that in my previous two classes, it was not that the examinations were adequately long that the students were able to finish them on time; it was simply because the B or C students simply gave up. In my current class, the B or C students did not give up. Most of them actually knew how to do the problems but they were not solving them as fast as the A students. Thus, in exam 2, I cut it short. I believe that I did not make it easier in terms of difficulty. I only took out several sub-parts of similar problems to the past examinations. As a result, the students did much better, more than 10% better than those in my previous two classes.

However, in exam 2, I gave two "application"-type questions where students were required to think, recognize the problem, find the solution, and apply it. Specifically, the questions were about induction, proof, and combinatorics. In the past, many students did poorly in both, not able to show their thought process correctly, the approach correctly, the problem solving strategies, and so on. It is definitely not so this time around. Many more students showed me that they were able to come up with some strategies (logical) to solve the problems. Even though they did not get the correct answer, they showed me what I have been preaching all semester long: problem-solving skills! So, even though I am not really happy about the high average and high median of my exam 2 this semester, I am very happy that the students learn more and show what they have learned in the examinations.

Use Student Feedback

Your students can also provide feedback to help you assess their learning and improve your teaching. Student evaluations are one source of this feedback, but targeted evaluation forms tailored to your course can give you more specific information about both attitudinal changes and suggestions for improvement, as Stu discovered (Exhibit 3.16).

Exhibit 3.16 Stu's Use of Student Feedback

One assignment that has helped me improve this course is having the students write an assessment of the course at the end of the semester [portfolio has a hyperlink to this student evaluation writing assignment]. The assignment is mandatory and graded on content. I ask the students to assess the course in their own opinion, including any negative feedback, in the form of constructive criticism. I ask them to evaluate the text, the course content, the teaching method, and what they were able to derive from the course. Since the assignment is graded, the students take more time and put more effort into it, plus they appreciate the opportunity to openly voice their opinions. Since doing this, I have received a lot of valuable insights into what the students felt was valuable, what they felt was busy work, and what they would like to see more of. After becoming involved in the peer review process, I found these student evaluations to be an extremely useful tool for me in assessing what the students had learned, and what I needed to work on more.

More importantly, it showed whether the students enjoyed the class, and whether they personally felt they had gained something by taking it. Since planning and scheduling is going to be a major component of their careers, it is critical they not only enjoy the process, but understand the importance of being able to do it well. By reading through the student evaluation letters, one will be able to see how the students were able to foster an interest in the subject, which they intend to further develop. This to me is possibly the most important outcome and assessment I could expect.

While I mentioned earlier that I do not feel it is necessary to teach the use of scheduling software, some of the students strongly disagreed in their evaluations [portfolio has a hyperlink to the student evaluation data], and would like to see more of it. Knowing they feel this way leads me to consider how to incorporate it a little more strongly without forfeiting the importance of scheduling by hand. While that was the single biggest criticism, it was interesting to read all of the evaluations to better comprehend how receptive the students are to learning the subject.

As these many and varied examples show, teachers can use a broad range of material to document and analyze student learning. The common factor in all these examples, however, is the teacher's reflection on the quality and quantity of learning that took place in his or her course.

Assembling the Portfolio: Link the Memos Into a Portfolio

The final step in writing your portfolio is connecting each of the three benchmark memos and placing the whole into a larger framework by means of an introduction and conclusion.

Introduce the Course Portfolio

Most teachers use the introduction to describe their own objectives in writing their course portfolio. You may find, as LeenKiat did, that as you work on your course portfolio your objectives become more specific and limited, and, therefore, attainable (Exhibit 3.17).

Exhibit 3.17 LeenKiat's Course Portfolio Introduction

Initially, when I first participated in this peer review of teaching (PRT) project, for the assignment memo 1, I started out with a host of objectives, mainly to document and capture students' and my enthusiasm, inquisitive activity, and effort. (Please see Appendix D in my portfolio for the initial set of portfolio objectives.) I have since realized, during the course of this PRT project, that the set of objectives was too ambitious. Thus, I have reduced the objectives to the following:

- I would like to document how students improve during the semester, based on their performance on the examinations, by specifically focusing on three students and then on the entire class in general.

- I would like to analyze how students handle different types of examination problems, specifically those involving problem solving (as opposed to knowledge recall or comprehension).

- I would like to compare students' performance on the examinations with student performance in the past classes that I have taught.

- I would like to provide this documentation for use in the future by other instructors for this course.

- I would like to hold myself accountable in the way I specify course goals and whether I measure for those in my examinations and whether students achieve my coarse goals.

Finally, I foresee using my course portfolio to document my teaching, to refine my courses, to disseminate to other colleagues, and to prepare for my promotion and tenure process.

Another option is to use the introduction to alert your readers to background information that you did not include in your course overview, as Nancy does (Exhibit 3.18).

Exhibit 3.18 Nancy's Course Portfolio Introduction

Textiles, Clothing, and Design 413 is designed to enhance students' ability to understand and attempt to solve critical problems relative to the merchandising of textiles and apparel products and related services. Enrollment is limited to thirty-five students to allow 1:1 computer access. This course has been taught for more than eight years as the capstone course for all TCD majors. Beginning in Spring 2005 this course will be required for only students with emphasis in merchandising.... Because TCD 413 is the third and final merchandising-based course in the merchandise major's program, accomplishing a high-level performance is an important outcome.

The creation of the College of Education and Human Sciences in fall 2003 has generated a stronger focus on communities, families, and schools. The content of TCD 413 previously focused on large industry, international trade, and global product sourcing. With the new college goals in mind, this course will align its focus on small communities and small business owners while delivering concepts related to the global economy.

In addition to the peer review team concept, TCD 413 was redesigned with input from two textile science masters' students in the department. Both hold B.S. degrees in merchandising from UNL [University of Nebraska–Lincoln] and have taken this course as undergraduates in 2002. They offered insight from the students' perspective for all assignments, quizzes, and grading rubrics. During the first semester their work in setting up the new course concept was conducted as independent study. The second semester's work was conducted as a teaching practicum. They assisted in development of the case studies, specifically taking leadership for case studies 1 and 5. They also developed and presented lectures on international sourcing and textile production, incorporating their current graduate work in textile science. They also assisted students in their online search for international sourcing information in case study 5, requiring communication with the U.S. Government's web masters.

Close the Course Portfolio

The conclusion gives you the opportunity to reflect on what you have learned, both specifically through your analysis of your students' learning and more generally as a result of writing your course portfolio. How close did your students come to attaining the goals for learning that you set for the course? What changes do you plan to introduce to the course the next time you teach it? Does your investigation of student learning have broader implications for your department's curriculum? What have you learned about yourself as a teacher in the process of writing a course portfolio?

Although they benefited in different ways from writing their course port-folios, both Wendy and Kathy attest to the value of the experience for their own professional development. For Wendy, writing her portfolio changed her perception of herself as a teacher (Exhibit 3.19).

Exhibit 3.19 Wendy's Reflections on the Course Portfolio

The process of constructing a course portfolio has shifted the ways in which I think about teaching and how I approach my role as the instructor. Prior to the process of writing the course portfolio, I was the typical instructor who focused much more on how I delivered the course material and was less attuned to the ways in which students receive the material. This is not to say that I spent little time thinking about my teaching, to the contrary as a junior professor new to the classroom, I was quite consumed with my performance in the classroom. The lens I used to evaluate my performance was strictly from the perspective of my delivery. With the peer review of teaching project, I have become much more concerned with how students are learning.

In addition, I have become much more in touch with the goals I have for students. I have also come to value the importance of explicit goals and objectives for my courses. Though I continue to struggle with articulating the goals versus the objectives for student learning, I am much more conscious of the importance of stating the explicit goals and objectives and holding myself and the students accountable.

I am convinced that this project has improved my teaching and provided me with some insight into how to evaluate my teaching beyond standardized student evaluations. The strategies and approaches to teaching were certainly a great benefit to this course, but I think my other courses benefited this year as well, as I was eager to implement the tips shared by my colleagues during the project. This project eroded some of the isolation associated with teaching. It allowed faculty members a space to dialogue about teaching and to share our classroom successes and failures in a safe environment.

Finally, this process has encouraged me to approach my teaching in the way that I approach substantive questions in my field using a deliberative, criti-cal, systematic analysis. In fact, the portfolio has prompted me to think critically about how students learn in women and politics courses across the country. Likewise, I am interested in how women and politics instructors and instructors of other courses that address sensitive material concerning race, class, gender, for example might use group processes as a means of alleviating some of the tensions that may arise concerning such topics.

Kathy's reflections on student learning confirmed her course goals, but they also suggested several specific changes she plans to make in how she teaches the course. Additionally, they have prompted her to consider larger issues of curricular change (Exhibit 3.20).

Exhibit 3.20 Kathy's Reflections on the Course Portfolio

Planned changes

As a result of participating in the peer review process I plan to maintain my current course goals and learning objectives. I also, though, plan to make several adjustments in the course materials, methods of delivery, and course activities so that students' day-to-day experience of the course might align better with the course goals. First, I am planning on experimenting with the use of several new exercises for comparing, contrasting and analyzing multiple theories of organization. These include the categorizing grid, and the defining features matrix (Angelo & Cross, 1993). I also plan to incorporate the pro and con grid (Angelo & Cross, 1993) to help students systematically critique these theories. Second, I plan to convert the in-class, case analysis writing assignments to homework writing assignments, primarily to allow more class time for the discussion of similarities and differences in students' application of theories to understanding and addressing organizational communication problems. In the future, I also plan to make greater use of the "lingering questions" exercise to get immediate feedback from students on concepts which remain unclear following lecture/discussion.

In addition, as a result of participating in the portfolio process, I am entertaining the idea of revising our curricular offerings in organizational communication and proposing a series of courses that would build upon each other more effectively. A 300-level course in organizational communication would address the foundational theories of organization and communication (classical, human relations and resources, and systems approaches), while the 400-level course would address cultural and critical theories of organizational communication. The 300-level course would require students to conduct an analysis of an organization as a communication system, while the 400-level course would require students to create an interpretation of an organization's culture.

Writing a course portfolio may seem like a daunting task. We are trained in graduate school to write about our research, but most of us have little experience writing about our teaching. But these two forms of writing are not so very different. Just as we are the experts in our particular area of research, so there is no one better qualified to write about the courses we teach than we are. And just as any research project becomes manageable when it is divided into smaller steps, so the task of writing a course portfolio becomes less intimidating when we break it into component parts.

And the effort is worthwhile. Almost all the faculty who have written a course portfolio at the University of Nebraska–Lincoln feel that the process has helped them improve their teaching not only of their target course but of their other courses as well. The formulation of course goals, the description of instructional practices, and the documentation and reflection on student learning in one specific course are powerful tools to make us more aware of our effectiveness as teachers.

What's Next

The five benchmark portfolios highlighted in this chapter illustrate the intellectual work of teaching in all its complexity as it is carried out in a specific course over the course of a semester. Sometimes, however, the process of writing a course portfolio raises more specific questions about particular teaching practices or issues that a teacher might want to address in depth. In these cases he or she might choose to write an inquiry portfolio that focuses on those issues. This is the topic of our next chapter.

4 Inquiring Into Specific Aspects of Teaching: The Inquiry Portfolio

Now that you have explored the process of creating a benchmark portfolio in Chapters 2 and 3, you might wonder, "What's next? What do I do with my portfolio when it's finished?" What happens next depends, of course, on your initial purposes for developing the portfolio. If you are interested in having it externally reviewed for a summative purpose, such as a promotion and tenure file, you might now turn to Chapter 5. But writing a portfolio may have caused you to ask new questions about your course. For most teachers, creating a benchmark portfolio is a powerful formative process that highlights issues central to their teaching goals that they hope to study further in future offerings of the course or in their teaching more generally. For instance, a teacher in special education and communication disorders said that the knowledge she gained from the benchmark portfolio process fostered further inquiry into her teaching:

> Through writing my benchmark course portfolio, two things happened. One, it solidified for me some of the different ways I've looked at my teaching over the years and said "that's an acceptable way to do it." Second, it extended my abilities by teaching me new ways to look at it. It provided me an opportunity to look at my class as a total product versus a linkage of separate topics and modules. As a result, the class has changed dramatically this fall as compared to how I was teaching it a year ago. And all

of it I can directly relate to my portfolio analysis. I reorganized the objectives or goals of the course; I developed rubrics for the assignments; I took study guides per topic and turned them into repeatable quizzes; I changed the assignments and made them more concrete. I increased the students' responsibility for reading. I've also changed my course evaluations. Additionally, I have also made an effort in this course to change my role from content specialist to facilitator. I don't know that I'm succeeding entirely, but I'm at least conscious of what efforts I'm making, and I have now formulated questions and issues that I want to change when I teach it next year.

For many instructors, creating a benchmark portfolio often leads them to continue studying issues in their teaching. Or as another teacher said, "Once you've started peer review, you can't stop."

In this chapter, we explain how you can further document and assess the intellectual work of your teaching through an inquiry portfolio. We developed the inquiry portfolio in response to the teachers who said that they wanted to take their peer review experience to the "next level." While a *benchmark* portfolio represents the overall goals and practices for a particular course, an *inquiry* portfolio is focused around a specific question or issue regarding teaching practices, course structures, or student learning over time. An inquiry portfolio helps you to investigate questions about your course that you really care about, that cycle back into your teaching for improved student learning, that are embedded within your local classroom context, and that you have encountered over two or more course offerings (Walvoord & Anderson, 1998). An inquiry portfolio also can be used to identify questions in your teaching that are applicable to teachers in the same discipline at other schools.

The Inquiry Portfolio

Instructors typically write an inquiry portfolio after they have created benchmark portfolios or after they have become experienced in reflecting upon and analyzing their teaching practices in a systematic and ongoing manner.

While a benchmark portfolio provides an overall portrait of how students are meeting goals and objectives within your particular course, the inquiry portfolio is usually focused on a particular issue or question that you want to investigate in teaching a course, often over several semesters. The advantage of writing a benchmark portfolio for a course before writing an inquiry portfolio is that the former often generates questions you want to explore in your course and provides a gauge from which to explore the impact of changes. In other words, the intellectual work produced by your benchmark portfolio is represented by the set of questions or issues that can be addressed by further inquiry into your teaching. However, you do not necessarily have to go through the process of creating a benchmark portfolio in order to develop an inquiry portfolio. If you have already identified a specific question about your teaching that you want to examine in a systematic and sustained way, you are ready to undertake an inquiry portfolio.

Since an inquiry portfolio focuses on a single issue in your course (rather than surveying an entire course), it is typically shorter than a benchmark portfolio. Like the benchmark portfolio, you build an inquiry portfolio by writing and sharing three memos with other teachers. However, the inquiry portfolio invites teachers to move more fully toward what some call scholarly teaching. Randy Bass's (1999) much-cited essay, "The Scholarship of Teaching: What's the Problem?" describes scholarly teaching as "not merely the existence of a scholarly component in teaching, but a particular kind of activity, in which faculty engage, separate from the act of teaching, that can be considered scholarship itself" (p. 2). For Bass, teaching is an activity that unfolds, apart from the physical classroom space, and encompasses the following:

> a broad vision of disciplinary questions and methods; . . . the capacity to plan and design activities that implement the vision; . . . interactions that require particular skills and result in both expected and unexpected results; . . . [and] certain outcomes . . . [that] necessitate some kind of analysis. (p. 2)

For some teachers, the questions they ask of their classrooms directly connect to disciplinary questions in their field:

> I believe teachers should ask questions about their students' work that grow out of their theoretical background; they should read and engage their students' texts by asking of them the same kinds of questions they ask of the scholarly texts they read and write. In addition, they should question the theories they espouse in terms of how they affect and reflect their students' learning. These are, for me, ways of nurturing and disseminating the scholarship of teaching and learning. (Salvatori, 2000, p. 84)

Other instructors focus more squarely on specific classroom practices, particularly in terms of their value for the learning that teachers hope to promote. In *Becoming a Critically Reflective Teacher,* Stephen Brookfield (1995) suggests that one purpose for teacher inquiry "is to question assumptions and practices that seem to make our teaching lives easier but actually work against our own best long-term interests" (p. 8). As faculty participants in our project have found, the initial investment of time spent developing an inquiry portfolio often leads to revisions in their teaching that yield much greater returns in the long run.

In this chapter, we describe the different steps for undertaking an inquiry portfolio and showcase examples from four teachers in different disciplines who have used the inquiry model to investigate a specific question in their teaching. Dana Fritz's portfolio for perceptual drawing examines the impact of three assignments that she revised on the basis of her benchmark portfolio. Christine Marvin's portfolio compares student performance and satisfaction in a graduate course in special education taught both on campus and through distance education. Tim Wentz's portfolio analyzes student performance in a new multidisciplinary architecture/construction management course and compares the "real time" students with those in the "TV" audience. Amy Goodburn assesses the impact of restructuring her reading theory course for pre-service English education teachers around a key concept. These examples will illustrate that while the steps for creating an inquiry portfolio are the same, teachers ask very different types of questions and use diverse methods for carrying out their investigations to best meet the needs of their student populations and their specific disciplinary communities.

Inquiry Memo 1: Stating the Issue or Problem to Investigate

Whatever the course, the steps of the inquiry portfolio model are generally the same. The first step is to identify the questions and issues that are most central to your teaching. In conjunction with your syllabus, you write a reflective memo about a specific problem or issue that you hope to investigate in your course, discussing why this issue is significant for your students' learning. This memo is typically two to four pages long.

It's important to remember that we are using the term *problem* in the way that Bass (1999) uses it, as a site for inquiry and research. Your focus might be on an issue that you've faced consistently in teaching this course (e.g., ensuring all students participate in a group project, or assessing the difficulty level of your examinations) or an issue that is often raised in disciplinary conversations about teaching similar courses (e.g., the impact of textbook supplements such as web pages and animations on student learning or the success of a particular curriculum for helping students succeed on national board exams). For instance, a professor in the School of Natural Resources used his benchmark portfolio to explore the success of a semester-long team project composed of undergraduate and graduate students grouped separately. His inquiry portfolio conducted a follow-up study to test the impact of mixing undergraduate and graduate students on these teams. Exhibit 4.1 provides prompts to assist you in considering possible questions you might wish to explore in your course.

Exhibit 4.1 Prompts for Writing Inquiry Memo 1

Course history and development

1) What is your course about and what is the institutional context surrounding it? If you are writing about a course for which you have not written a benchmark portfolio, you may want to refer to the questions for the Benchmark Memo 1 to offer some context. Some questions you might consider: What is the course? What are its goals? Who are the students? What is your teaching history in relation to the course? How long have you been teaching it? What role have you played in developing it?

2) Describe a timeline or sequence of stages for how the course has evolved (in terms of course goals, assignments, pedagogical strategies, etc.). How have you viewed its success with respect to student learning? Have you made changes to it during successive course offerings? How would you assess the usefulness or success of these modifications?

Identifying an issue to investigate

1) What is an issue or problem you hope to study in this particular course? Why is it useful or important for you, as a teacher, to investigate this problem? How might investigating this issue contribute to your students' learning, your own professional development, and/or to the scholarship of teaching in your field?

2) What do you know about your students' learning that makes this issue important to investigate? What do you know about the curriculum that makes this issue important to investigate and address (e.g., course is a prerequisite for other courses, course is a capstone of the major)? How does this issue respond to or address larger conversations about the undergraduate (or graduate) student experience at your school? How does this issue connect to larger conversations in your discipline or field that makes it important to investigate?

Examining issue history and significance

1) When did you first observe this issue/question? What are some sources or explanations for it (e.g., student preparation, curricular fragmentation, teacher experience, institutional context)? Have you taken any steps to address the issue already? If so, what were these steps and what were the outcomes? (If you have sought to address this issue over successive course offerings, provide a timeline or sequence of modifications that you have made to address the issue.)

2) Is this question or issue represented or taken up by students within the course directly? Are there readings, assignments, or course activities through which students engage in this issue/problem? Describe the ideal outcome(s) you believe would be achieved if this issue were addressed or solved within this particular course.

If you are struggling to think of a central question to study, you might find it useful to return to your benchmark portfolio as a starting place for such inquiry. Oftentimes the benchmark portfolio brings to the surface questions or issues that teachers can then develop more systematically for study. In other words, by providing a snapshot of overall student performance in your course, a benchmark portfolio often helps teachers to identify specific areas in their courses that they wish to improve upon. For instance, Dana used her inquiry portfolio as an opportunity to continue studying her students' work in her perceptual drawing course. Exhibit 4.2 illustrates how Dana sought to analyze the effectiveness of new assignments that she developed as an outgrowth of writing her benchmark portfolio.

Exhibit 4.2 Dana's Inquiry Portfolio Goals for "Perceptual Drawing"

My inquiry portfolio analyzed three new assignments I added to the course in order to increase the students' understanding of perceptual drawing techniques. In addition, two of the assignments are designed to make the students' drawing progress more explicit for their own evaluation as well as mine as their instructor. The data I analyzed included student work and excerpts from their reflective writing about the work.

As a result of last year's work with the Peer Review of Teaching program, I made a few changes to my perceptual drawing unit that include additions and alterations to assignments and objectives.

- I added a planar analysis assignment in which students analyze complex three-dimensional forms and break them down into planes in order to draw them. First they complete a planar analysis drawing of their face and later they build a life-size planar faceted mask of their face based on observation and their drawing.

- I added a new set of assignments that function like a "pre-test" and "post-test" to measure student learning in a visual way. On the first day of class, I assigned a 2–3 hour self-portrait from observation (using a mirror). The students were free to use any media from the provided materials list and reminded not to draw from photographs. This drawing marked each student's incoming level of drawing ability before my instruction. At the end of the unit, they were given the same assignment again. This drawing was intended to measure the students' ability to synthesize and apply what they have learned in the way of materials, techniques and concepts. Analyzing the two drawings side by side gave my students more information for their own written reflections on their progress in my class. It also helped me to evaluate their progress for a grade.

Dana's inquiry portfolio gave her a way to systematically document the effectiveness of the new assignments as well as to analyze the pre- and post-test measures she developed on the basis of her benchmark findings. Christine also designed her inquiry portfolio to document the impact of changes that she made to her course based on her assessment of student performance in the benchmark portfolio. Christine teaches a course that enrolls two sets of students: on-campus students and distance education students who never physically meet with her. While Dana created three new assignments to better match what she identified as her course goals for perceptual drawing, Christine did not change the overall structure of her assignments. Instead, she was interested in revising and refining the assignments that she already used in order to make more explicit her standards for performance and to promote higher levels of student responsibility for their own learning. Christine also hoped to examine whether student performance between the on-campus and distance students differed in any measurable way. Exhibit 4.3 illustrates Christine's multiple goals.

Exhibit 4.3 Christine's Inquiry Portfolio Goals for "Issues in Early Childhood Special Education"

I was eager to teach this revised course. I intended to evaluate this course for its own merit as well as seek a comparison with data and student outcomes from my previous year's offering of it. Specifically, I aimed to answer three questions:

1) Can distance and campus students perform equitably on course assignments despite variability in access to the instructor?

2) Will modifications in course design (methods and measurement) result in satisfactory student evaluations and learning outcomes for the majority of students?

3)   Will final grades reflect the range of abilities and efforts of the varied student types enrolled in the course?

Similarly, Tim sought to compare student performance between two different student populations—students who attended his "live" class versus students who attended the "television" class that took place at the same time on a different part of the campus—for a brand-new course that had been developed in collaboration with two university colleges. Beyond documenting his own effectiveness as a teacher, Tim desired to use his inquiry portfolio as scholarly evidence to both colleges that this new course could work and that student learning could be enhanced in this new format. In Exhibit 4.4, Tim describes the institutional and economic pressures to develop this new course as well as his own commitment to ensuring that the course is successful for both student populations.

Exhibit 4.4 Tim's Inquiry Portfolio Goals for "Building Environmental Technical Systems"

This new course was created when two existing courses were merged: one offered by the Department of Architecture in the College of Architecture and one offered by the Department of Construction Management in the College of Engineering and Technology. Anticipating the current budgetary crisis sweeping higher education, the two colleges met to identify courses that could be combined into a single course that could be taught once a year in a large-class format. From this review, "Interior Architectural Systems," a course taught in the architecture college, and "Physical Environmental Systems," a course taught in the construction management department of the engineering college, were selected for consolidation into one large, multidisciplinary course.

From the standpoint of the two colleges, the purpose of the new course was to reduce the teaching load within both colleges. However, from a teaching perspective, it was my opinion that a highly technical course could be effectively taught in a large-class format. Moreover, it was also my opinion that combining architectural students and engineering students in the same learning environment would produce a synergistic environment wherein learning could be enhanced. Therefore, my objective in selecting this course for my peer review course portfolio was to produce the scholastic documentation necessary to prove the accuracy of my opinions.

While Christine's and Tim's inquiry portfolios focus mainly on the institutional pressures that shape their courses and the student populations within them, Amy's inquiry portfolio focuses more on disciplinary issues and questions that shape how she constructs the course and promotes student learning. Amy examined how pre-service teachers demonstrate their conceptual understanding of social location—how social differences such as race, class, gender, and religion shape students' reading and writing in high school English classes. Exhibit 4.5 illustrates how Amy used her inquiry portfolio to engage in the move between theory and practice that Salvatori (2000) calls for, to take up disciplinary questions by examining how students engage in these questions through their learning.

Exhibit 4.5 Amy's Inquiry Portfolio Goals for "Reading Theory and Practice"

This portfolio describes and assesses the impact of revisions I've made to English 476, "Reading Theory and Practice," over the past four years and is a follow-up to the benchmark portfolio I developed for it. In the benchmark portfolio, I sought to provide a complete description of the 476 course goals and activities and to demonstrate student learning within the course. In this inquiry portfolio, I describe how I have revised the syllabus in terms of course goals, assignments, text selections, and class activities using the concept of "social location" as a framework. I examine how the concept of "social location" served as a lens for students to examine and theorize their own and others' reading histories within formal writing projects and class activities. I also examine the usefulness of modeling specific pedagogical practices (such as double-entry diaries and criteria-generating activities) as a way of helping students conceptualize and theorize models of instruction for their future teaching of reading. Because I've substantially revised the course each time I've taught it, this portfolio does not provide a body of student work that can be compared across courses (because project assignments have varied). Instead, I have included syllabi for three different years so that readers can see the course's evolution in terms of goals and overall design.

As these examples show, the format of an inquiry portfolio is broad enough to accommodate a wide range of issues and goals, yet the specific portfolio is designed to focus the reader's attention on a small and well-defined question or set of questions.

Inquiry Memo 2: Generating a Hypothesis and Developing a Methodology

Once you have developed a question or issue that you'd like to systematically study, the next step is to generate a provisional hypothesis and develop a method that will enable you to inquire into its usefulness. While writing Inquiry Memo 2 does not require a formal research study such as one typically undertaken in academia, this memo does ask you to propose a methodology for investigating the problem or issue that you identified. What, specifically, do you plan to change or study in the teaching of your course (e.g., specific methods, course materials or assignments, assessment of student work)? What do you predict will be the impact of such change? How will you collect data to test this impact? This memo is typically three to six pages long.

You might be thinking, "How can I generate a hypothesis when I do not have a background in educational research?" As we discussed in Chapters 1 and 2, it is important to remember that our model for peer review of teaching does not require a doctorate in educational research. Rather, we share the belief of Glassick, Huber, and Maeroff (1997) that research into one's teaching parallels the methods of inquiry that researchers normally use (clear goals, adequate preparation, appropriate methods, significant results, effective presentation, and reflective critique). In other words, it is important not to lose sight of the goal for an inquiry portfolio—to answer meaningful questions that you have about your teaching. Given that, it can still be valuable to peruse existing literature on teacher development. For instance, Angelo and Cross (1993) outline more than 50 different techniques that teachers can use to collect data on their classes, including informal writing, surveys, checklists, and inventories. Many of these techniques are useful not only for answering a hypothesis in an inquiry portfolio but also for providing you with concrete feedback about student performance and understanding that you can use *as you are teaching*. And of course you can always draw upon the research practices used within your specific discipline. For instance, Amy's and Dana's portfolios employ mainly qualitative approaches to inquiry because both of them are working within an arts and humanities tradition. Christine's and Tim's approaches are more quantitative, using charts and numbers to represent student performance on different measures. Your main goal in developing a hypothesis should be to state a claim that you feel is valuable to "test out" in your classroom. Exhibit 4.6 offers prompts that can assist you.

Exhibit 4.6 Prompts for Writing Inquiry Memo 2

Defining a hypothesis

Convert the issue you identified in Inquiry Memo 1 into a provisional hypothesis or generative statement that you hope to prove or understand more deeply through your inquiry. Have you framed an issue or a set of questions that can be productively studied in the course of a semester? In exploring this issue, are there one or more alternative hypotheses that you might consider? Which hypotheses will be most useful for improving student learning?

Developing methods of inquiry

1) What do you think it will take to research or understand this issue more deeply? What do you already know about the issue that will assist you in investigating it? What do you need to know further about the issue in order to address it? For example, if your problem is motivating students to prepare outside of class time, what do you know about how they currently prepare for your class? Is it an issue of time? Experience? Ability?

2) What classroom evidence or (qualitative and quantitative) data will help you to understand and/or address the issue you have identified more fully? Can your hypothesis or provisional statement be answered or proved with specific, observable phenomena from the classroom? If so, what phenomena might that be? How might you go about collecting this data or observing the phenomena that you need to further your investigation?

3) What other resources or avenues might provide you with useful information for studying or addressing this question/issue (e.g., student surveys, secondary reading of pedagogical literature, interviews with colleagues)? What difficulties do you anticipate in studying this issue? How might you connect this inquiry with your students' learning?

Data collection

1) What are the independent variables and dependent variables for testing your hypothesis? Independent variables are those that you as teacher have influence over (e.g., amount of homework you assign). Dependent variables are those that you are seeking to measure (e.g., average exam score).

2) How do you envision sampling? What will be the duration of data collection and the time interval (e.g., daily, weekly)? What is your sample size? Why do you feel this particular sampling will provide you with the data you need to prove your hypothesis?

3) What assumptions do you have to make in regard to your hypothesis (e.g., your presentation style will be similar as a previous semester's, or your student population generally remains the same across repeated course offerings)? Are there assumptions that you can test via your data collection? How might you go about doing so?

For the teachers described in this chapter, the hypotheses or provisional statements varied widely both in terms of scope and number. For instance, Christine developed a list of teaching goals that she hoped students would accomplish in her course. Rather than developing hypotheses that she wanted to test, she turned what she hoped to see with respect to improved student achievement into a list of goals that she could measure in a quantitative way throughout the semester (Exhibit 4.7).

Exhibit 4.7 Christine's Teaching Goals

---

1) Students will show improvement (grades/scores) in professional writing skills from Module #1 to Module #4. *(>50% of students will show grade increases of at least one-half point on graded 1500-word paper from Module #1 to Module #4)*

2) Students will be able to justify recommended practices in ECSE [early childhood special education] and show ability to integrate information about laws, research, and recommended best practices across topics or modules presented in class. *(80% of students will show grades of 3.0 or better on two or more 1500-word papers; at least 25% grades to be 3.5 or better)*

3) Students will demonstrate an ability to critically read textbook chapters and research articles across the term. *(80% of students will receive grades of 4.0 on at least 6–11 reading reviews)*

4) Students will develop and modify a philosophy statement regarding their views for early childhood special education that reflects knowledge of theory, research, and federal/state laws. *(80% of students will draft a philosophy statement by mid term and revise it at least once by term's end. >50% will show evidence of theory, research, and/or laws in their final philosophy statement)*

5) Students will demonstrate knowledge of laws and basic terms and facts related to early childhood special education. *(80% of students will score at least 80% or better on 8–10 quizzes)*

While Christine developed her goals for her inquiry portfolio around objectives that she had identified as important to her teaching, Tim's generated hypotheses developed, in part, from his colleagues in the colleges of architecture and engineering. Because he was teaching a new course born out of a collaboration between the two colleges, Tim's portfolio outlined the institutional decisions that had been made for him in developing this course, including which texts he could use and specific course content that had to be covered (Exhibit 4.8). These institutional pressures were important for Tim to document because they necessarily shaped and informed the hypotheses that he could generate about student performance within the course.

Exhibit 4.8 Instructional Factors Shaping Tim's Course Design

During the original discussions with the architecture department, a number of meetings were conducted to discuss course content, pedagogical strategies, prerequisites, course goals and other issues relating to the structure of the course. Obviously, there existed a significant difference in perspective on the overall goals of the course. However, it was my opinion, shared by professors in both architecture and engineering, that this particular course could be effectively taught and even enhanced by changing its structure to a large-class format in a multidisciplinary environment. This became my working hypothesis for the course portfolio. Through these discussions between the colleges, we reached the following compromises:

- Building-sustainability and energy conservation topics would be incorporated into the course to a greater extent than currently provided by the construction management department.

- The text on heating, ventilating, and air-conditioning (HVAC) systems used by the architecture department would be retained.

- The text on plumbing systems used by the construction management department would be retained.

- The course name would be changed to "Building Environmental Technical Systems."

- The course prerequisites of physics and calculus would be retained.

- A recitation section would be added to the course allowing problem solving and hands-on applications.

- A requirement to develop three-dimensional "drawdels" (half model, half drawings) would be incorporated into the class.

In contrast to Tim's and Christine's quantitative approaches for documenting and assessing student learning, Amy used more qualitative methods to examine how the concept of social location informed her students' understandings of how to teach reading and writing. Amy's portfolio was also explicitly designed with an eye toward contributing to conversations with disciplinary colleagues beyond her institution. In Exhibit 4.9, Amy outlined her hypotheses and questions that she would like readers of her portfolio to consider regarding her overall curricular goals and the ways that the inquiry portfolio demonstrates scholarship into her own teaching. Because Amy was interested in disseminating her model for teaching reading theory and practice through journal articles and a book on preparing English/language arts pre-service teachers, she was more interested in soliciting feedback about the larger conceptual underpinnings of her course than in focusing on specific course practices and assignments.

Exhibit 4.9 Amy's Hypotheses and Questions Posed to Readers of the Portfolio

Based on external reviewers' comments to my earlier benchmark portfolio, I refined my course objectives and tied them more concretely to course assignments. For this portfolio, I've chosen to assess the impact of these changes via a close analysis of student work. To carry out this analysis, I initially developed three hypotheses about my course objectives:

1) The concept of "social location" helps students to better understand pedagogical and theoretical issues involved with why, how, and what students read. It is useful to have students apply this concept via a case study of readers' engagements with texts.

2) Modeling reading strategies within the classroom and having students reflect upon the usefulness of these strategies better prepares them to conceptualize models for their future teaching of reading.

3) Focused attention to how assessment criteria are generated and used can help students assess their own written work and help them to understand the relationship between assessment and curricular planning for their future teaching.

As a reader of my portfolio, please focus on the following questions:

*   Does the overall design of [English] 476 with respect to the concept of social location make sense in terms of introducing pre-service English education students to pedagogical and theoretical conversations about the teaching of reading at the secondary level?

*   Do the assignments and class activities I've profiled seem valuable for helping pre-service teachers develop an understanding of reading theory and practice?

*   Does the design of this course portfolio demonstrate a useful example of scholarship into one's teaching? Are there significant gaps or areas that I need to consider in representing my scholarly inquiry into the teaching of this course?

In sum, the hypotheses you generate for your inquiry portfolio should enable you to answer a significant and focused question in your teaching.

While the answers to your hypotheses are valuable in helping you to restructure or revise the way you teach a particular course, they also might benefit other colleagues both within and beyond your institution.

Inquiry Memo 3: Analyzing and Assessing Your Findings

Once you generate a hypothesis that you want to investigate for the inquiry portfolio, your next step is to determine what type of data you need to collect. Like the memo that we described for benchmark portfolios in Chapters 2 and 3, this inquiry memo focuses on actual classroom data and student work. Bass (1999) notes: "It takes a deliberate act to look at teaching from the perspective of learning. Actually, it takes a set of acts—individually motivated and communally validated—to focus on questions and problems, gather data, interpret and share results" (p. 2).

In this memo you analyze and reflect on the data that pertain to your classroom issue or hypothesis. If available, this data can be compared to what you have collected in previous offerings of the course. If you are interested in documenting changes in student performance in your course over time, for instance, you might focus on a set of assignments or projects that students complete throughout the semester and use that to compare student performance in several iterations of a particular course. You could compare students' response to an essay exam over three course offerings to determine if there are improved scores after you have developed and shared better paper grading criteria. Or you could compare student performance on a midterm exam for students who completed web-based practice exercises versus those who did not. If you are interested in studying how well students perform on higher-order exam questions as opposed to rote memorization questions, you might focus on collecting all of the exams for your course and doing a detailed breakdown of how students did both individually and as an aggregate on the different categories of your exam questions. If you are interested in studying how students employ a particular concept, you might think about collecting a wide variety of student assignments in which these concepts are incorporated. Or you could evaluate a student team project along with students' perception of the project, their team interaction, and their project quality for exploring the impact of how teams were formed. The possibilities are endless. Thus the method of data collection you use will necessarily depend on the context of the course you are teaching and the hypothesis that you've generated to study. Exhibit 4.10 offers helpful prompts for writing this memo.

Exhibit 4.10 Prompts for Writing Inquiry Memo 3

Interpreting your data

1) What does the data you have collected tell you about the problem or issue you originally chose to investigate? Does the data indicate your initial hypothesis is supported? Does the data suggest that your initial hypothesis might be incorrect? Do you see a new hypothesis emerging with respect to the issue you hoped to address? Are there new issues or questions emerging from the data that you hadn't considered or that help you to reframe the issue(s)?

2) How has studying this issue or question affected your teaching of the course? How does the student work you've collected speak to or illustrate the significance of the issue you are studying? What does your data analysis tell you about how students are learning? Is there evidence that the modifications you made have improved students' learning/performance as represented in their work samples? Does student learning/performance indicate that they have a better understanding or appreciation of the issue that you identified? Did students achieve the outcome you hoped for?

Disseminating your analysis

1) How might you best represent and disseminate your findings to others via your inquiry portfolio? Can you document the demonstrated impact of the modifications you made in your teaching this semester? For example, did the range of distribution regarding student performance on a particular assignment improve? Could you represent this improvement via a graph or a pie chart in comparison with previous course offerings?

2) Which artifacts from your students' work demonstrate or illustrate improved student learning? How might you share these findings (e.g., reflective summaries on passages from student papers or a statistical summary of students' improved test scores)? Which artifacts raise questions or issues for further study?

Future inquiry and development

1) Overall, did your investigation help you to better meet your students' learning needs? Based on your data analysis, what changes do you plan to make in this course to help students achieve? Are there particular features of the course that you would redesign? What specific changes do you plan to make in how you teach or organize the course? How do you think these changes will improve student understanding? Do you see a need for curricular, programmatic, or departmental changes based on your investigation?

2) How do the findings from your inquiry contribute to your own professional development and/or to the scholarship of teaching within your field or discipline? How did the process of collective reflection with other advanced program participants help you in understanding the issue(s) you chose to investigate?

Clearly, the data you collect must help you to answer your original hypothesis or any new hypotheses that have emerged during the course of your inquiry. For instance, Dana's data collection involved digitally photographing student artwork. Dana was interested in documenting student performance on the three new assignments that she was piloting, and so she focused her collection on these three projects rather than all of the projects that students completed in her course. Because Dana's benchmark portfolio illuminated the value of having her students write reflections about their art processes, she also collected students' written reflections on their art and the processes they used to produce it. The first class assignment was a self-portrait that was to be used as a pre-test of students' drawing skills. On the last day of the eight-week course, Dana assigned students this same project, creating a post-test evaluation of students' growth in drawing skill and their reflective analyses of their growth. Exhibit 4.11 illustrates how this activity was valuable to Dana for evaluating student performance and for students in self-assessing their growth in drawing skills.

Exhibit 4.11 Pre- and Post-Test Self-Portraits From Dana's Perceptual Drawing Course

Hypothesis: The pre-test and post-test self-portrait drawings are intended to measure the students' ability to synthesize and apply what they have learned in the way of materials, techniques, and concepts. Analyzing the two drawings side by side will give my students more information for their own written reflections on their progress in my class. It will also help me to evaluate their progress for a grade. (Grading art is so subjective that a strict structure like pre-test/post-test is a welcome addition to my evaluation process.)

Student Rosey: "I think that my recent self-portrait is a lot more accurate than my first. Many things were wrong with my first, whereas the new one really looks a lot like me. The composition in itself is also very intriguing compared to the first. The first had no frame and wasn't anything interesting to look at. The new one has 'narrative potential' and a frame that sets it off."

Student Li: "It is surprising how well my drawing turned out. I'm pretty sure that it is because of what I have learned in the past few weeks. My second self-portrait became more accurate (because of Sighting), more real and more three dimensional (because of Value exercises)."

Student Christopher: "Based on the range of thought that went into my first self-portrait and the thought that went into the more recent one, it is obvious that I'm more visually literate. I gave a lot of thought to the composition, transition of values, lighting and the use of the page. Drawing another self-portrait actually made me wish I'd concentrated more on the first and considered those concepts. Since the first, I've bettered my ability to use those ideas without thinking as much."

To assess her hypotheses regarding the second new project—a 3D planar analysis assignment—Dana also showcased student work and students' written reflections about their processes. In Exhibit 4.12, we can see Dana's ongoing teacher reflection as she continues to think about how she will revise the assignment in the future. For instance, she comments on the fact that she was unable to collect students' written reflections on the three art pieces she documents because she didn't require students to turn in their edited reflections. Thus she identifies a change she will make in future offerings of the course. She also notes an appreciation for the difficulty level of this assignment and her plans to provide students more time to complete the task in the future.

Exhibit 4.12 Student Work for Dana's 3D Planar Analysis Assignment

Student Lynette: high-pass grade   Student Rosey: high-pass grade

Student Joe: low-pass grade

This assignment was extremely challenging for almost all students but the majority of them learned quite a bit by doing it. Not only did they learn to solve craft and structure problems, they also honed their observation skills, which will help them in subsequent assignments. Their reflective comments indicated that they learned about the relationship between 2D space and 3D form. I don't think I gave enough class time to this difficult assignment in the past and have decided to give students an entire week with a weekend to complete it.

The following comments are from students' reflections on the 3D planar analysis assignment. I do not have comments from the students whose masks are pictured because those students did not choose to include their mask comments as part of the edited reflection they turned in to me. In hindsight I see that I should have been more explicit about addressing each project in their typed reflections. However, I think the comments below represent the feelings of many students in the class.

Student Barbara: "Planar analysis also helped, but in a different manner. By translating 3D into 2D and then taking that 2D drawing and putting it back into 3D, as we did with our masks, I was forced to treat the subject matter differently. Instead of defining an object by its curvature, I was forced to relay its curvature through angles. It was a different and extremely challenging process."

Student Kristin: "I also enjoyed the mask project. Although it was difficult and time consuming, it taught me a lot about the facial structure, mostly in the cheekbone region. I believe that this aided me in my final portrait because I was able to distinguish which areas of my face needed the most contrast for better definition."

Student Laura: "After practicing hours upon hours of organizational line drawings, a 2D Planar Analysis was to be drawn of our faces. I thought this task was easy. It's easy for me to think in 3D and draw it on a flat surface. When it came down to actually constructing the mask, I found it more difficult than expected."

Student Desiree: "The faceted mask was also very productive. I had to have the dexterity to take what I observed on my face and mimic it on my mask. This was one of the most difficult things I've had to do. The challenge taught me patience and made me improve my observation and craft skills."

Beyond "testing" the value of the new assignments that Dana incorporated into her course, she also learned through the inquiry portfolio process how to be more objective in the ways that she evaluates student performance. The written criteria Dana delineated for each project based on her benchmark portfolio enabled her to articulate clearer expectations for her students' work. These criteria also enabled her to state more specifically in her hypothesis for the inquiry portfolio what she wanted to study about her students' performance for the three new activities.

Christine's data collection focused on student work as well, although her approach was markedly different from Dana's. To answer her hypotheses, Christine designed an evaluation that students completed after finishing each of the four modules in her course as well as after the course as a whole. Christine also drew upon her students' final course evaluations to answer one of her hypotheses regarding students' attitudes toward her course. While both Dana and Christine analyzed student work to answer their questions, Christine's approach was decidedly more quantitative. Exhibit 4.13 illustrates the various ways that Christine collected and analyzed data to answer her set of hypotheses.

Exhibit 4.13 Christine's Data Collection

In order to evaluate the impact of the changes I made in my course, the following assignments were reviewed over time:

- Reading reviews
- 1500-word papers
- Quiz scores
- Posted philosophy statements on Blackboard

The first three assignments (reading reviews, papers, and quizzes) were available for each of four modules in the class. So every 4 to 5 weeks of the course, I summarized the students' abilities and used the class data as a reference for subsequent module assignments and summaries. I also had students complete a course/teaching evaluation after Module #1 and Module #3 to explore specifics regarding student impressions about:

- Usefulness of assignments and various course activities
- Their own "learning-to-date"
- Applicability of course for meeting listed course objectives
- Their desire for more or less structure in the class

Similar to Christine's data collection, Tim also analyzed examination performance for the two student populations that comprised his course. But in his portfolio, Tim also used qualitative inquiry to examine student projects for a service learning component in which students recommended renovations for a local church. Like Dana, Tim used a digital camera to photograph the students' "drawdel projects" (half models/half drawings) that depicted their proposed church renovations in graphic form. Tim described three different types of evaluations. From a quantitative standpoint, he analyzed the examination performance. From a qualitative standpoint, he analyzed the student projects. Finally, from a quasi-quantitative standpoint, he analyzed the student evaluations.

Exhibit 4.14 shows Tim's reflection on his students' examination #2 performance for each section of his course. A similar analysis was done for all three examinations in the course. Exhibit 4.15 shares Tim's reflection on the student evaluations of the course. Exhibit 4.16 highlights the student projects.

Exhibit 4.14 Tim's Exploration of Exam Scores

A reduction in the number of failing grades did occur in examination #2. However, unlike examination #1, a differentiation in performance between the students in section 001 (live lectures) versus section 002 (broadcast lectures) is evident. For the first time, I am observing data that does not support my original hypothesis. I also observed that although the standard bell curve is still present in the data, I notice a clumping of grades inasmuch as there are no grades of A-, B- or C-. In all honesty, I have no idea why that would be the case as the examinations are multiple choice and each examination is comprised of 30 questions. At this point in the semester the data raises a concern that the students in the remote classroom are not learning at the same rate as the students in the live classroom. In an attempt to react to that observation, I tried to ask more questions of the students at the remote classroom and I tried to sharpen my skills at using the remote cameras, so I could physically focus in on the students either asking questions or responding to questions. In short, I was trying alternative strategies to better incorporate the students [in the remote classroom]. . . . At this point, I am still not convinced that the students at the remote site are not learning at the same rate as the students listening to the actual lecture. However, it is clearly a possibility.

Exhibit 4.15 Tim's Reflection on the Course Evaluation

The following graph represents the teaching evaluations from both section 001 (live) and section 002 (remote).

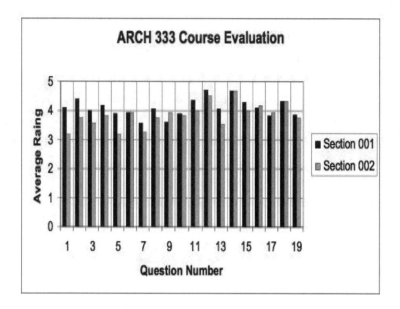

As can be seen, the evaluation of the students in section 002 is lower than section 001, yet both sets of numbers are well above average. Even though the perception of learning, as seen by the students, indicates that the learning was not as pronounced in the remote site, one can conclude from this data that both sets of students were generally satisfied with the course, its format, and the way it was taught.

In looking at this data, I am not sure it supports my hypothesis directly, either. Said another way, it appears to me that the students are reacting favorably to the course content and the way it was taught, though there is less satisfaction at the remote site. I do think this data indicates that the students are not biased towards the broadcast technology, which was one concern I had in developing the course. In fact, one of the reasons we decided upon using a Polycom system was the ease with which we could focus on the remote site with the remote cameras and exchange a visual presence.

Additionally, I think the data shows that the students are generally aware of the extreme financial challenges currently manifesting themselves in academia.

In fact, we discussed this at some length at the beginning of the class. As we move to do more with less, it will be necessary to use larger classes and broadcast more classes to more remote sites. I have found that being honest and upfront with the students about what you are doing and why you are doing it will generally result in a greater understanding of the process and, accordingly, a greater degree of acceptance. This data, to me, speaks to that understanding.

Exhibit 4.16 Tim's Student Projects

The first goal of this course was to teach the students the language of mechanical systems so that they could converse intelligently with those professionals responsible for designing and constructing mechanical systems. The second main goal of the course was to learn how and why mechanical systems work. The real heart of this course, the third goal, was to teach the students how to apply the basic fundamentals of mechanical systems to the built environment. The mechanism I used to evaluate this process was the semester project.

If there was one area of this course that was an unqualified success, it was in the performance of the students on the semester project. As described previously, the students were divided into multidisciplinary teams comprised of two architecture students and two construction management students. Each team had to write a 10-page report identifying the problems faced by the church and their recommendations to overcome the problems using the most energy efficient and sustainable processes available.

The semester projects were uniformly outstanding. Better yet, the students recognized their efforts as outstanding, as did the church. One student told me after the semester ended that she had never put so much time into a semester project in her college career. At the same time, without any comment whatsoever from me, she also remarked that she was really proud of how well her team had done.

The following photography illustrates the quality of the projects:

In looking at the grades earned in each section, I was not able to discern any significant difference between the two sections. Based upon the semester project alone, I would conclude that the student learning did not vary significantly between the two sections. The difficulty in using this statement is that it only focuses on the performance of the team, not the individual. In order to ascertain the performance of each member of a team, I used a grading rubric that required each student to grade their own performance and the performance of each of their team members. This data did not identify any differentiation between the student performance in the live site or the remote site.

Unlike Tim's portfolio, which focused on a brand-new course in the engineering curriculum, Amy's portfolio focused on the changes she has made to her reading theory course over a four-year period. Because one issue that external reviewers commented on in her benchmark portfolio was the appropriateness of the course texts, Amy created a table in her inquiry portfolio to represent the changes she has made in selecting course texts along with written rationale for why these course selections were made in relation to her changing course design (Exhibit 4.17).

Exhibit 4.17 Changes in Text for Amy's Course Over Four Years

First Year	Second Year	Third Year	Fourth Year
Sula	On Reading	Mosaic of Thought	Reading Don't Fix No Chevys
In the Middle	Envisioning Literature	A Classroom of Teenaged Readers	A Classroom of Teenaged Readers
Oxford Book of American Short Stories	The Giver	I Read It, but I Don't Get It	I Read It, but I Don't Get It
	Reading Strategies and Practices	I Hear America Reading	I Hear America Reading
		The Prairie Schooners	The Prairie Schooners
			40 Short Stories
			Packet of prompts, student examples, and extra readings

Beyond analyzing her own pedagogical choices, Amy also focused on student work to answer her larger question regarding how the concept of social location was used by her students to understand reading and writing practices. Unlike Tim's and Christine's use of charts to track students' numerical grades, Amy drew upon three students' case study projects and closely analyzed places in these projects where the students employed the concept of social location. Exhibit 4.18 represents her analysis of one student's project, with her commentary surrounding excerpts from the student's writing.

Exhibit 4.18 Amy's Analysis of Student Application of Theory in a Case Study Project

Tracy's project was one of six projects that represented "excellent understanding." In addition to eight typed pages about her readers, Tracy's project included seven appendixes of supporting material such as the survey instruments and interview questions she used to carry out her project. The following excerpt demonstrates Tracy's ability to analyze her reader's engagement with texts in terms of class concepts:

> Jalaina's positive reaction to *House on Mango Street* suggests that teachers can use their knowledge about students' likes of texts to recommend and refer students to other literature. Zirinsky and Rau state in *A Classroom of Teenaged Readers,* "we believe teenagers have similar experiences when they read works they like, and it is the kind of connection they seek in assigned reading." Jalaina made me realize that educators have an important responsibility to nurture students' habits by providing links from a student's favorite books to other texts. Jalaina was able to make important inferences about Cisneros' short story based on other reading experiences. This is an excellent example of an enriching literacy moment in the seen text.

Tracy's project also uses specific examples and details from the protocol to fully represent how her reader engaged with the text and to consider how the reader's social location might be shaping her experience with the text. She writes:

As a student at a parochial school, Jalaina questioned the text from her experiences with the nuns at her school. In response to the nun in *House on Mango Street* commenting negatively on the narrator's home, Jalaina wrote: "I go to a Catholic grade/high school so I know about nuns. They aren't supposed to put people on a pedestal for having nice things or make people feel bad for lack of possessions." Jalaina related to the text based on her understanding of the roles of nuns. She used an interactive voice, when reading the nun's dialogue aloud, and made faces in response to the nun's negative comment. When she reflected her thought processes, she questioned why a nun would have the audacity to judge a young girl's home.

Tracy's understanding of reader theory is further illustrated when she provides an overall summary of how her reader makes sense of texts. Her use of specific terms, such as "inferences" and "story-driven texts," demonstrates her ability to apply class concepts in this specific context.

Whatever form of data collection and analysis you choose to use, your main goal is to answer the important questions you have about your teaching of the course. How you choose to represent these answers will necessarily be informed by the approaches that you use in your disciplinary field and by the nature of the data you have available to collect and study from your course.

Overall Assessment of the Inquiry Portfolio Process

As with a benchmark portfolio, an important part of an inquiry portfolio is the section in which you reflect on what you have learned through the process of writing the portfolio. Christine looked at the entire two-year process of writing first a benchmark and then an inquiry portfolio (Exhibit 4.19). Her investment in the process resulted in an increased satisfaction with how she taught the course and answered her questions about the possible disparities between on-campus and distance-learning students.

Exhibit 4.19 Christine's Reflections on the Inquiry Portfolio Process

I am very pleased with the changes and outcomes in my course. The quizzes, rubrics, module questions and methods/activities for engaging students on-and off-campus have clearly paid off in more advanced understanding of the issues associated with practices in early childhood special education (ECSE). More importantly, the understanding demonstrated by most students in this most recent offering of it suggests a comfort with the information and an ability to relate various facts (terms, theories, laws, research findings) to the design of quality ECSE programs. Not only do I feel better about my efforts to expose students on-campus and at a distance to the literature and laws associated with ECSE issues, I am pleased with the evidence of their integration of the readings, class notes and class discussions. I see now the value in writing assignments addressing higher-level questions over lower-level review questions/exams.

The two-year process was worth the time commitment. I have such a greater appreciation for my students and the efforts they put into classes and the frustration they feel when a class is poorly organized or assignments are not relevant or clear. The peer evaluations and discussions in the first year of the peer review project forced me to look at aspects of my course I would otherwise have ignored due to ignorance about their importance (i.e., rubrics) or my own fear of facing errors and poor quality performance on my part. The data collection during both years, although more extensive than I plan to do in the future and far more than many peers pursued, was necessary for me. Even in reviewing the course in 2002, I felt the need to look deeply at examples and analyze patterns that went beyond my initial set of review questions. I had learned the value of such time commitments in the Year 1 portfolio process and knew that I could likely learn something of value following such analyses. And I did.

Because Tim was teaching a brand-new multidisciplinary course in a televised format, his reflections are important not only for his own teaching but for his colleagues in both departments. In Exhibit 4.20 Tim's excerpt also illustrates that the process of inquiring into his teaching directly impacted his students because he made his inquiry visible to them and invited their participation and reflection about the course structure and design.

Exhibit 4.20 Tim's Reflections on the Inquiry Portfolio Process

Inasmuch as this course was my first attempt at teaching a large-format class I think I was bound to learn a great deal over the course of the semester. Additionally, this was also my first attempt at teaching both a multidisciplinary course and my first attempt at broadcasting a course. Even considering all of the newness experienced in one class, I came away very enthused about the potential of large-class instruction. In many aspects, I believe that the large-class format can be superior to smaller classes although I also recognize that this is only true for certain types of classes. I believe that the highly technical course I taught this past fall is an ideal candidate for large-class instruction as long as a recitation section is built into the class to allow for one-on-one problem solving.

I also learned that students are generally very resilient and actually quite forgiving. We spent a considerable amount of time at the beginning of the course talking about what we were attempting and why we were attempting it. We also made time throughout the semester to assess what was working and what wasn't working. The feedback was generally constructive and, to some extent, I think the students then developed some ownership of the course. This is probably the single most important reason the class succeeded.

The portfolio process allowed me to develop a cogent course structure and evaluation process to enable and quantify student feedback. It is doubtful that the students would have taken such an ownership position in the class without the portfolio process to guide its formation.

Like Tim, Dana acknowledged the value of the peer review process for her students, as they learned to reflect on their own improvement over the eight weeks of the course (Exhibit 4.21). She also recognized that writing an inquiry portfolio helped her to see how assessment of student work in a discipline that is usually considered subjective could be more objective and rigorous.

Exhibit 4.21 Dana's Reflections on the Inquiry Portfolio Process

Producing an inquiry portfolio gave me a framework in which to refine my course. Although the methods I used seemed at first too scientific for a subjective area like art, the "Hypothesis, Data, Conclusion" structure allowed me to be more objective about my teaching. It is all too easy to get caught up in the personalities of students or blind arrogance about the quality of my work in the classroom. The more scientific structure allowed me to consider my preconceived notions about what I hoped would happen, look at student work as raw data and analyze the situation to come to an informed conclusion. The rigor of this structure kept me on track and provided a system for documenting student work and reflective comments. I plan to continue using this structure in some form to further refine the course each semester.

Participating in the Peer Review of Teaching Project has helped me to write better curricula and more fairly evaluate student learning. The reflective writing process required for peer review was so useful it inspired me to assign it to my students as well. The reflective writings seem to keep them more intellectually engaged in work that can sometimes be quite technical. They also seem to help students understand that they *are* making progress even if their drawings aren't the best ones on the wall. In an eight-week course, it is difficult for students to step back and understand what they have learned. Their reflective writing practice complements their intense drawing and promotes a more complete understanding of their work and progress.

Amy's reflections on the inquiry process also focused on ways that she plans to continue revising her course. She identified specific changes she plans to make to her reading theory course in connection with pedagogical approaches and disciplinary texts in her field. Amy's reflections also returned to her initial goal of developing an inquiry portfolio that can be read and reviewed in terms of scholarship of teaching in her discipline. Exhibit 4.22 notes that she viewed her portfolio as an opportunity to engage in conversation with English/language arts teachers beyond her institution.

Exhibit 4.22 Amy's Reflections on the Inquiry Portfolio Process

In general, I was pleased by student performance on the three formal writing projects, particularly the interpretive narrative project. Next year, though, I have decided to eliminate the third project, a multi-genre research project, so that I can make the interpretive narrative project the culminating project of the semester. This move will provide students more time, enable them to apply all of the reading theory concepts we've learned instead of those just at midterm, and enable me to discuss more fully how the project is connected to principles of teacher research. One issue that I noted is that some students viewed the interpretive narrative project as a pedagogical practice itself rather than a form of research into reading pedagogy. That is, some students said that they wouldn't do an interpretive narrative project with students because it would take too much time. In introducing the project next year, then, I need to do a better job of contextualizing it as a form of teacher research, similar to the research represented in *Reading Don't Fix No Chevys*. Instead of a third writing project, I am considering developing guided small reading groups in which students would read a common book on some aspect of reading theory and practice. While the multi-genre research project enabled students to pursue questions related to reading instruction, the individual focus did not lend itself to cross conversations (beyond the final class presentations). Instead, I plan to have small groups of students read a common text, providing some in-class time for discussion of the text and perhaps for a collective class presentation about the text in thinking about issues related to reading theory and practice. This project would also model how they can organize reading instruction that allows student choice rather than requiring all students to be reading the same book at the same time.

Even though I wrote a course portfolio about [English] 476 three years ago, writing this inquiry portfolio was still a challenge. Based on reviews I received to the first portfolio, I wanted this portfolio to more adequately represent the type of work my students engage in, the ways I respond to their work, and the global issues that I view as important for this course to take up. As a faculty member interested in and committed to inquiry into the scholarship of teaching, I want this portfolio to represent the type of inquiry that will lead to ongoing conversations with others involved in English/language arts teacher education. While I feel this portfolio illustrates how I have revised and refined ENGL 476 to better introduce students to central issues in reading theory and practice, I am interested in hearing other readers' responses. Like the ENGL 476 course itself, I view this portfolio as a constantly evolving text to which different readers will bring different and multiple meanings and insights. I look forward to hearing others' readings of this portfolio and continuing the discussions that this inquiry portfolio process has fostered.

While the four teachers profiled in this chapter wrote inquiry portfolios for different purposes on courses that varied widely in terms of course content and student population, all of them found their experiences valuable and worthwhile. Moreover, all four have used their inquiry portfolios—in varying ways—to contribute to larger conversations about teaching issues in their disciplinary fields, moving toward the scholarship of teaching paradigm. Tim, Christine, Dana, and Amy have presented papers based on their portfolios at conferences in their respective disciplines, and they have continued to actively use and advocate for peer review of teaching methods in their departments.

What's Next

This chapter has focused on helping you to investigate and study a specific aspect of your teaching through the structure of an inquiry portfolio. All the teachers we have profiled found writing such a portfolio useful in understanding and improving their teaching of a specific course. But the benefits of participating in peer review are not limited simply to improving one's teaching of a particular course. In the next chapter, you will read about other reasons that teachers value their participation in a community focused around structured reflection on and analysis of teaching.

5 SOLICITING AND WRITING EXTERNAL REVIEWS FOR COURSE PORTFOLIOS

As we have suggested throughout this book, teachers find course portfolios to be a valuable medium for documenting their teaching so that it is available for peer review and assessment. Since portfolios can be read, evaluated, and used by others, they also offer mechanisms for valuing teaching as scholarship. Lee Shulman (1999) asserts that the scholarship of teaching "makes our work public and thus susceptible to critique. It then becomes community property, available for others to build upon" (p. 16). Unfortunately, most national and campus teaching efforts focus primarily on persuading faculty to participate, with little attention to creating mechanisms for evaluating and assessing the work resulting from this participation. In other words, while many schools are creating communities of teachers engaged in documenting their teaching, not many schools have equally nurtured communities of readers to assess and value this work. To accomplish Shulman's vision of circulating and using scholarship about teaching, we focus on the external review of course portfolios.

The external review of a course portfolio is the next step in the process: You make your teaching available for public use and assessment. Similar to the external review of a scholarly publication or grant application, a portfolio review is a reader's written assessment of your portfolio. A reviewer can either be internal to your department, program, college, or university or external to your school. This chapter focuses on the uses of external reviews for course portfolio authors. In conceptualizing the external review process, there are two significant questions to address: "How do I go about reviewing a peer's course portfolio?" and "What are the issues involved in eliciting a review of my course portfolio?" This chapter addresses each of these central issues.

Formative and Summative Evaluation

A *formative review* is for portfolio teachers who wish for low-stakes feedback on their teaching practices as represented in the portfolio and an outside evaluation of how well the portfolio presents an argument or offers evidence for their teaching. Thus a formative review is usually written for the portfolio author. Soliciting a formative review is analogous to sharing the draft of a scholarly publication with a colleague before submitting it to a journal editor. Also similar to a formative review of scholarly research, the review process for a course portfolio can be helpful to both authors and reviewers, prompting fruitful exchanges about teaching within and across disciplinary communities.

In comparison, *summative reviews* typically focus on whether the course portfolio provides evidence of high-quality teaching, whether the course design and goals reflect national standards within a disciplinary field, or whether students' performance is representative of national norms. A summative external review is typically written for a person or group making a decision about the portfolio's author. As a dean of arts and sciences once told us:

> I'm most interested in the summative review, a review that will hold weight when a faculty member goes up for promotion to full professor. I need a review that provides evidence that the professor's teaching makes a national contribution to the field.

In this respect, the summative review is often used in high-stakes decisions about one's teaching and is generally solicited and read by colleagues rather than by the portfolio author. Often the reviewer's name is not shared with the author.

For the Portfolio Author: Soliciting a Review for Your Course Portfolio

Since teaching is typically a private activity, usually only observed by a limited number of peers and rarely by anyone outside your university, seeking an external review can be anxiety producing. We are rarely asked to document our teaching in such a visible way. For many faculty members, the act of writing a course portfolio is benefit enough, without the additional layer of having it reviewed. But for others, having one's portfolio externally reviewed offers valuable feedback, confirmation, and inquiry into one's teaching practices and approaches. Just as you may have multiple purposes for creating a course portfolio, you may have many different purposes for soliciting an external review of your work. To begin the review process, it is important to specify your goals for the review, both in terms of the type of review you want and the types of reviewers from whom you need to solicit.

Before soliciting an external review, we suggest sharing your portfolio informally with colleagues first, as a test run. You might ask a faculty member outside your department to provide you feedback as well. Such a process can help you to identify issues or questions that readers outside your institution might have about your course and can allow you to fine-tune the overall presentation of your portfolio before it is disseminated to external reviewers.

Type of Review

The first step of an external review is to identify what type of review you are seeking: formative or summative. Are you looking for feedback that would help you to improve your teaching or the way you document and describe your teaching in the course portfolio? Or do you need a more formal evaluation of your course portfolio, the course design, and the resulting student learning?

Type of Reviewer: Disciplinary or Nondisciplinary

We find it useful to think of reviewers in two categories: those within the portfolio author's disciplinary field and those who are outside the author's area. Both have their advantages, particularly if the author is interested in eliciting a formative review that will aid in the further revision of the course portfolio. The advantages of a disciplinary review are obvious, and many of the teachers we have worked with say that getting feedback from a peer in one's discipline is critical.

A disciplinary peer in communication studies reviewed a teacher's course portfolio and was able to directly respond to the challenges that the author identified in teaching her students. Indeed, the reviewer suggests that the teacher's challenges are reflective of the discipline of communications studies and not a "fault" of her pedagogical expertise:

> [The teacher's] primary concern, encouraging students to fuse theory with practice, is a common "problem" for communication studies faculty. One of the discipline's fundamental challenges during its contemporary history has been to respond to the recurring expectation held by the academy, the workplace, and students that communication courses teach communication skills. Put simply, communication studies is a discipline that carefully negotiates communication theory with communication practice. In this portfolio, [the teacher] demonstrates how this mission operated as the framing principle for her entire organizational communication course.

This excerpt illustrates the value of having an external reviewer, who is also a disciplinary peer, comment on the intellectual work of one's teaching. The reviewer's comments suggest that the pedagogical concerns that the teacher identified are not individual to her teaching but rather are indicative of disciplinary concerns that many faculty face in the field of communication studies. This type of assessment cannot be generated from student evaluations and would probably not surface in a peer observation in the classroom. The reviewer provides the disciplinary expertise of a faculty member who is current with the intellectual content of the discipline and can comment on the appropriateness of particular course design features.

The advantage of a review by a nondisciplinary peer might not be so apparent. You might wonder, "How can a faculty member who has never taught the same course possibly understand the challenges I face or the decisions that

I have made?" True, a faculty member in history might not be able to comment on how well a course represents disciplinary concerns in mathematics, for instance. Yet a reviewer outside your discipline can offer a useful perspective. Such a reviewer can generate ideas and see outside the disciplinary "box" in ways that colleagues within your field cannot. For instance, if you are developing a course portfolio to help support your promotion and tenure materials, you might want to gain a sense of how the portfolio will be read by faculty across your institution, since this same cross-section of faculty will probably serve on the college committee that reads and evaluates your files. In this case, a reviewer outside your discipline might identify places in your portfolio that rely too heavily on disciplinary jargon or that assume readers share the same assumptions that you do regarding values and goals for learning in a particular discipline. For instance, when a colleague's portfolio in English education was reviewed by two English professors, two English education professors, and a faculty development coordinator of a teaching and learning center, she received dramatically different assessments regarding her course structure and design. Some of her reviewers questioned her course readings; others focused on her classroom activities. While the author found the disparity of reviews initially dizzying, she gradually understood the value of having those both inside and outside her field review the course:

> I realized the extent to which I was being asked by the reviewers to argue for, rather than simply describe, the pedagogical goals and practices I supported. Reading the external reviews invited me to consider the implications of these different reviewers' perspectives and how they represented institutional and disciplinary assumptions about what constitutes effective English teacher education.

Once you determine whether you want a disciplinary or nondisciplinary reviewer (or both), your next step is to identify possible reviewers.

Who Should Review?

If you want a formative review, you might contact peers at other institutions where you know a similar course is being taught, or you might rely on colleagues whom you have met at disciplinary conferences. If you need a summative review for a course portfolio that you plan to submit with a promotion and tenure file, your department colleagues will probably identify one or more reviewers. Although this approach is similar to the current processes routinely used for reviews of published scholarship, there is a key difference. While reviewers for traditional scholarship are usually experts who have already published within the particular discipline or area, a reviewer of a course portfolio may have never authored a course portfolio (or even seen one before). In these cases, it is especially important that you provide department colleagues with clear directions and criteria that they can share with potential reviewers.

Additionally, the status or ranking of a school can be an important issue for a summative review. For instance, many academic departments require external review of promotion materials to come from an identified list of "peer" schools. Yet the local needs and interests of schools can be central to how one documents teaching in ways that do not compare to traditional scholarship that is "transportable" or the same across school contexts. For instance, if a first-year sociology course incorporates a community service-learning component, reviewers might need to be chosen on the basis of their expertise in service-learning rather than sociology. Some schools offer journalism courses through the English department, while others offer journalism courses within programs in broadcasting and media. Selecting a reviewer for a journalism course, then, might require some additional investigation into the reviewer's institutional context and the ways that the overall programmatic goals for the teaching of journalism might differ. Or to consider some other scenarios, what if the course you are teaching is not taught at your peer-identified school, or, if it is, what if you know that the teacher who commonly teaches the course at the equivalent school is not a successful teacher? Or what if a course that you teach for an English department is taught, instead, within an education department that values different approaches and holds competing assumptions about the nature of student learning? What if the author and reviewer teach the same course at very different kinds of institutions, with different resources for faculty and different expectations of faculty?

Those choosing external reviews also must make other decisions. For example, should a summative review of teaching be given more weight if it is authored by a teacher who has developed his or her own course portfolio, won a teaching award, or has been named a Carnegie Teaching Scholar? While we do not have the answers to these questions, we think it is important for those selecting reviewers to be aware of them. At the University of Nebraska–Lincoln we ask portfolio authors to identify a list of external reviewers in their disciplinary area that they feel might provide useful feedback. We then contact these individuals and ask if they would be interested in writing such a review for the faculty member. We attempt to solicit a minimum of two reviews for each portfolio—one by a disciplinary peer and one by someone outside the area. You might be wondering if it is necessary to compensate reviewers for their time. Early in our project, we offered reviewers $100 for each written review. While this was a small thank-you to reviewers, we did not think it had much impact on the quality or quantity of reviews and discontinued the practice.

Providing Guidance for the Reviewer

If a person agrees to write a review, we send a formal letter providing directions for accessing the course portfolio, give a clear deadline for receiving the review, and include a copy of our reviewer guidelines to help them structure their review. Exhibit 5.1 illustrates the types of questions we ask reviewers to consider in four categories: course intellectual content, quality of teaching practices, quality of student understanding, and reflective consideration and development.

Exhibit 5.1 Outline for Reviewer Comments on a Course Portfolio

The following headings identify four major topics that could readily be part of an external review of a course portfolio. We encourage you to use these or similar headings to identify the portions of your comments related to these specific issues in teaching. You need not reply to all the prompts, but they are provided to begin your reflection on the course portfolio. Please feel free to make your comments in either a narrative format or as identified single sections. Any additional comments about the teaching represented in these documents would be welcome. Please feel free to expand on your reactions to the intellectual quality or effectiveness of this professor's teaching beyond the types of issues that we have posed. Remember that your frank but constructive reactions to what is presented will be very helpful in the development of the course and course portfolio. At the end, please include a few sentences that describe your experience in teaching courses related to the one you are reviewing. It is not necessary that you have taught exactly this course, by type or by content, but it is helpful to the author of the portfolio to know your experience.

Intellectual content of the course

Please evaluate the quality of the *course's intellectual content*. This may include but is not limited to:

- Appropriateness of course material both for the curriculum and the institution
- Intellectual coherence of course content
- Articulation of intellectual goals for learners and congruence of those goals with course content and mission
- Value or relevance of ideas, knowledge, and skills covered by the course

Quality of teaching practices

Please evaluate the *quality of the teaching practices* used in the course. This may include but is not limited to:

- Organization and planning of contact time; congruence between planned and actual use of contact time
- Opportunities to actively engage students in the material
- Opportunities (in or out of class) for students to practice the skills embedded in the course goals
- Particularly creative or effective uses of contact time that seem likely to improve student understanding
- Activities scheduled outside of contact time that contribute to student achievement (this may include extracurricular activities, group projects, electronic discussions, or any other planned course-related assignments or activities)
- Course structures or procedures that contribute especially to the likely achievement of understanding by learners

Quality of student understanding

Please evaluate the *quality of student understanding*. This may include but is not limited to:

- Appropriateness of student performance, in light of course goals, course level, and institution

- Performance levels that reflect challenging levels of conceptual understanding and critical evaluation of the material appropriate to the level of the course and of the students

- Appropriateness of forms of evaluation and assessment, given the stated goals of the course

- Creativity in providing students with ways to demonstrate their understanding of and ability to use the ideas and content of the course

- Alignment between the weighting of course assignments in grade calculation with the relative importance of the course goals

- Demonstration by an appropriate percentage of students that they are achieving competence in the stated course goals, or identification of reasons why they might not be reaching these levels of competence

- Revisions or modifications to the course that could improve performance

Evidence of reflection and development

Please evaluate the *evidence of reflection and development.* This may include but is not limited to:

- Substantive reflection by the faculty member on the achievement of the goals for the course

- Identification of any meaningful relations between teaching practice and student performance

- Evidence of changed teaching practice over successive course offerings in reaction to prior student understanding

- Evidence of insightful analysis of teaching practice that resulted from consideration of student performance

Reviewer's teaching experience in this area

What similar courses have you taught (i.e., class size, level, content)? Have you taught using a similar format (i.e., course structure, presentation format)?

A note to peer review project directors or departmental colleagues: Once we receive the completed review, we copy it (removing the reviewer's identity) and forward it on to the portfolio author. We send a formal thank-you letter to the reviewer. We encourage each author to write a response to the reviewer's comments, offering their reactions, insights gained, and discussing points with which they agree or disagree. In addition, we ask portfolio authors to assess if the review has been helpful, and if so, how. If not, we want to know why. Finally, we encourage and offer assistance to each portfolio author to update and revise the portfolio based on the reviewer's comments.

What to Do With a Review?

How can you most productively use the external reviews of your course portfolio? One question we are frequently asked is, "Should I respond in writing to the reviewer?" After all, a colleague at another school has generously taken the time to review your portfolio, so what is your obligation in responding to the reviewer? The answer to this question will depend on the type of review you solicited and the types of response you received in the review. If your goal was to receive a formative review, for instance, you possibly know the name of the reviewer and the review itself probably focused on concrete strategies for improving your course and perhaps sharing of ideas by the reviewer. In this case, you'll probably want to thank the reviewer for his or her suggestions and discuss how you have learned from the review.

You have important choices about using and responding to the review itself. For instance, if you are submitting a review as part of a promotion and tenure file, consider how you want to frame and use the review. Will you simply add it to the folders, similar to how most external review letters of scholarship are included, or will you write some reflective analysis of what you have learned through the review process? Should you respond in writing to the review, particularly if it critiques a particular component of your course design, to show the "uses" you have made of the review in your thinking and learning about teaching? Should you include the review(s) as an attachment to the portfolio, as evidence that it has been peer reviewed? Some of these questions necessarily depend on the school environment in which you are working. For instance, will external reviews be critically read in light of the institutional and disciplinary issues entailed in soliciting reviewers for a particular course? Only you can decide how to engage in and use the review process.

For the Reviewer: Reviewing a Course Portfolio

"I have written a course portfolio about my teaching and was wondering if you would write a review for it," asks a disciplinary colleague from another school. Your first response is to agree. But when you sit down to read your colleague's portfolio and write a review of it, you realize you have no idea what to do. Your reaction would not be unique. While we as faculty are well experienced in reading research and scholarship in the form of journal articles, book manuscripts, and grant proposals, we are often less practiced at reading and writing about a peer's teaching. This challenge is compounded when the portfolio you are reviewing is not in your disciplinary area. With a disciplinary review, you probably have the expertise to comment on the course's topics, goals, and text(s) even if you have not taught exactly the same course. On the other hand, with a review outside your discipline, your assessment will probably focus more generally on teaching practices across contexts and your colleague's representation of student learning in the presentation of the portfolio.

Just as the format of course portfolios can vary, the form and genre of the external review can also vary. For instance, you can write in a memo format, using headings and bullets to organize your response. Or you can write a letter that is addressed to the portfolio author or to the author's department chair. These differences in genre and audience speak to the two main types of reviews: formative and summative.

Know What Kind of Review You Are Expected to Provide

The first step in writing an external review is to determine what type of review you are expected to write. Beyond gauging your own disciplinary and pedagogical expertise, you should be clear about the purpose of the review. If not, discuss with the portfolio author or the person who contacted you how he or she intends to use the review. Does the author want you to write the memo directly to her, identifying problems and issues within her teaching that she can then work on? Or does she plan to send the review to a third party as part of a teaching award nomination or promotion and tenure file? The genre and form you use for writing the review will depend, in part, on the portfolio author's goals. Some teachers seek a formative assessment of their portfolio and are interested in a peer's opinions about the quality of work produced in their course. Other teachers wish to have their teaching reviewed for more summative contexts, such as tenure and promotion cases or teaching award nominations, which require more formal evaluative reviews.

You can benefit from the process of writing a formative review: Reading someone else's portfolio can help you think more critically about your own teaching of similar courses. Even if the course portfolio you are reviewing is outside your disciplinary area, some teaching issues will connect in some way to your own concerns—for example, lecturing in large classes or the effectiveness of using small groups. At the very least, when you read another teacher's course portfolio, you develop a better understanding of the complexities involved in documenting and representing student learning. Writing a formative review can offer you a space for engaging in a dialogue about your own teaching. Reviewers often describe their own course methods (assignments, teaching practices, assessment practices, etc.) as they respond to the portfolio author, offering suggestions for texts, projects, and overall approaches. And reviewers sometimes find that the portfolio author gives them new ideas for how they might teach similar subjects.

Components of an External Review

Once you have determined whether the review should be formative or summative, your next task is to create a structure for the review. Glassick, Huber, and Maeroff (1997) suggest that six criteria typically used for evaluating faculty research (clear goals, adequate preparation, appropriate methods, significant results, effective presentation, and reflective critique) can also be used to read and assess teaching as scholarship. With these criteria in mind, our approach has been to focus course portfolio reviews around four key issues: evidence of and quality of the course's intellectual content, teaching practices, student understanding, and reflection on one's teaching and course development.

The Course's Intellectual Content

The first part of your review should focus on an assessment of the course—its topics and goals. This component is particularly important if you share disciplinary expertise with the portfolio author or teach a course similar to the one you are reviewing. Common issues to discuss in your review might include the following:

- Do you agree with the topics covered in the course?

- Do you agree with the course goals?

- Is there congruence between course goals and course content?

- Does there appear to be an intellectual coherence to the course content and structure?

- Are the knowledge and skills covered by the course appropriate to the curriculum, level of course, institution, and/or national standards of accreditation?

Exhibit 5.2 showcases excerpts from course portfolio reviews that discuss the intellectual content of several different courses. As you read through these excerpts, you can see how the reviewers often draw upon their own teaching experiences and disciplinary understandings of the field to comment on whether the intellectual content of the course is both appropriate and effectively organized. For instance, in Exhibit 5.2, a chemistry professor affirms the course portfolio author's decision to revamp the course structure based on new discoveries in biology and biochemistry and suggests that the course's emphasis on "helping students learn how to learn" parallels his own teaching practices. The reviewer of the natural resource field science course portfolio notes that the course's primary emphasis on fieldwork gives its students a tangible advantage over other students nationwide in this disciplinary area. Similarly, the reviewer of the English education portfolio notes that the underlying structure of the course is developmentally appropriate in helping pre-service students examine their own reading practices and those of their future students. All these reviews offer praise for how the courses are intellectually framed and structured.

Exhibit 5.2 Review Excerpts Discussing Course Intellectual Content

- *From a review of a chemistry portfolio:* The portfolio author indicates that he had extensively revised the course offering and rearranged topics to allow for a slightly more thorough covering of the material. I wholeheartedly agree with this approach for a number of reasons. Firstly, our current understanding of biomolecules, especially protein and nucleic acid structure, has exploded in the past 5–10 years. Specifically the sequencing of the human genome has provided a wealth of information that is only beginning to be mined. Consequently, a good understanding of structure/function relationships of proteins and DNA will be increasingly important to researchers in the field of biology in general and biochemistry in particular. Secondly, I have seen the consequences of the condensed introduction to biochemistry that is endorsed by my school. Almost all of the students feel completely overwhelmed by the amount of information they are expected to assimilate (i.e., memorize). Increasingly, introductory biochemistry courses are the first synthesis course where information from basic biology, chemistry, physical chemistry, and physics all comes together. The amount of new information introduced in introductory biochemistry is such that only the very brightest of the students can fully integrate the information. I concur with the portfolio author that our role should be one of enablers helping students learn how to learn. We need to help them create their own mental framework on which they can begin to arrange the disparate information acquired in all of their courses. Only with a clear mental framework or map can they truly understand what they are learning.

- *From a review of a natural resource field science course:* This course is different from many college courses where the material is presented, the students are tested, and the course is over. This course requires that the students use the material to develop a product that has use for resource managers. Thus, the professor must not only teach the material, he must ensure the students learn enough of the subject so they can develop the product. This places a great deal of stress on both student and teacher. The author's approach seems to accomplish this task in an environment that is most useful to the student. He starts by letting the students determine what they need to know, shows them that they will learn it, and then provides feedback to them as they develop their soil map product. The course material is appropriate for the expected student outcomes. His objectives are most sufficient and articulated to give the student adequate insight into not only where the class is going but why. I find the course to be very valuable for all students who are planning to use the soil resource in their careers. This course will continue to remind them long after graduation of how important an understanding is of soil variability across a landscape. This is because they got out in the field and actually did it once, and the actual field work will stay with them. Field courses like this are not very common, and the students at this school who take this course will have an advantage over students at other schools who only do their "field work" in the lab or classroom.

• *From the review of a course portfolio in English education:* The teacher's approach in this course—its organization and content—seems well suited to this particular student population, the goals of the course, and the curriculum of which the course is one part. Reading becomes an unconscious activity for most people so the teacher's effort to defamiliarize (through reading a nonsense version of "Little Red Riding Hood") and bring a metacognitive perspective to the activity of reading seems an excellent beginning to this course. The application of this new awareness—first to a student's own reading and then to the reading practiced by actual high school students—is a logical extension of student learning. The course seems intellectually coherent, especially in her effort to "practice what is preached" and in the reader response theory that is embedded throughout.

Beyond affirming the intellectual structure of a course, external reviews also can offer specific suggestions for how to reconceptualize and reorganize a course for improved student learning. While some reviews offer a colleague's concrete suggestions regarding textbooks and course projects, others focus more broadly on how successfully the course's overall goals and objectives are articulated. For instance, in Exhibit 5.3, a political science teacher affirms the case study approach used by the portfolio author but suggests a new topic might provide more diversity for enhanced student understanding. In contrast, the reviewer of a nursing course portfolio critiques how the teacher "collapses" goals and challenges, suggesting that the course's goals might still be fuzzy, both to the teacher and the students within it. And a different reviewer of the same English education portfolio discussed above in Exhibit 5.2

presents a starkly different perspective on the intellectual coherence of the course's overall objectives.

Exhibit 5.3 Suggestions for Improving the Intellectual Content of a Course

---

- *From a review of a course portfolio in political science:* This course is well structured. I like the way the three case studies are integrated. I wonder, however, if it might be wise to substitute another country for either Rwanda or Sierra Leone. My reasoning is simple. While both represent good case studies, they are too similar. I would think that including a country such as Somalia or Sudan might be more useful. Why? Because the author would have (1) a country from black Africa, (2) one that is somewhat both black and Arab and in the case of Sudan, primarily Muslim, and (3) an Arab Christian/Muslim country. I realize that there may not be sufficient material available on these countries, but I think looking at one of them would help students better understand similarities and differences between the various countries.

- *From a review of a course portfolio in nursing:* I found the author's presentation of the goals of her course somewhat unclear. There seemed to be a concentration of "goals" and "challenges" with no clear distinction between the two. Are they the same thing or are they not? Are the challenges obstacles (or opportunities) in the path of achieving the goals? I believe this section of the portfolio could be improved by more clearly (and physically) separating the goals and the problems associated with achieving them.

- *From a review of a course portfolio in English education:* The four course goals listed in the syllabus seem to be too much about process for its own sake. In this way, they do not relate sufficiently to the "content" area specified twice . . . i.e. "what constitutes effective literacy instruction" and "what constitutes best practices in reading and writing instruction?" Two of the goals—"reflecting on their own and others' literacies" and "exploring what it means to be a teacher of English"— strike me as too vague to be meaningful.

These reviews offer several revision suggestions in terms of the course aims and goals but also in terms of the organization of the course portfolio itself. In the review of the nursing portfolio, for instance, the problem of confused goals might lie more in the representation of the teacher's goals within the portfolio rather than in the instructor's actual syllabus. Thus this reviewer's comments might be easily addressed through a revision of the portfolio's organization rather than an overhaul of the actual course design.

Quality of the Teaching Practices

The second section of a review typically focuses on an assessment of the teaching methods (course activities and course materials) used in the course. If you are writing a review for a portfolio outside your disciplinary area, this section will probably be more extensive than the previous section. While it may be difficult for you to comment on how a particular course's objectives "stack up" to national norms in the field, you may have much to say about particular teaching practices and strategies and their effectiveness in supporting student understanding. For instance, teachers of classes with more than 100 students often face common issues regarding how to engage students, how to track student learning, and how to best deliver course content. Conversely, classes with small student populations often share common issues regarding the use of small-group work, the integration of writing-intensive instruction, or promoting active discussions. Regardless of the teaching practices an instructor uses, common issues to discuss in this section of a review include the following:

- Are teaching methods appropriate to the level of the course?

- Does it appear that students are engaged by the course?

- Are there opportunities (in or out of class) for students to practice the skills embedded in the course goals?

- Are there particularly creative or effective uses of contact time that seem likely to improve student understanding?

- Are activities scheduled outside of contact time (e.g., extracurricular activities, group projects, electronic discussions) that contribute to student achievement?

- Do certain course structures or procedures appear to contribute to the student learners' likely achievement of understanding?

Portfolio authors often say that the teaching strategies section of the course portfolio is more difficult to write than the section on course goals and objectives, in part because this section focuses on how teachers engage in the delivery of course content. Similarly, reviewers of course portfolios often ask for a clearer picture of how class time is used, desiring more concrete and tangible representations of how teachers interact with students and sponsor their learning within the classroom. The following excerpts in Exhibit 5.4 illustrate how reviewers often draw on their own teaching strategies when they review colleagues' uses of instructional time. For instance, the reviewer of the English course affirms how the teacher uses supportive comments in responding to student writing, describing them as parallel to his own "rhetorical" approach. The reviewer of the political science portfolio not only praises the use of simulations for the course but offers his own strategies for ensuring that students make the best use of this pedagogical method. The reviewer of the English education course describes the range of teaching activities as diverse and clearly related to the instructor's goals to model valuable teaching techniques. The reviewer of the construction management course portfolio articulates a shared philosophy regarding the role of computer software programs in helping students learn.

Exhibit 5.4 Positive Review Excerpts Discussing Course Teaching Practices

- *From a review of a course portfolio in English:* The portfolio author does not over-correct student writing, avoiding the possibility of draining a student's enthusiasm. On the other hand, he is still teaching in his comments. He uses each student's observations to guide them to a greater understanding of the theory under examination. Even when presented with final drafts of student papers, I respond to student writing by suggesting further lines of enquiry. I emphasize to students that even though it is important to establish rhetorical positions in one's writing, it is also helpful to consider that processes of critical thinking can always be extended.

- *From a review of a course portfolio in political science:* I like the participatory/simulation part of the class. I have used similar practices and the students seem to like them. The key is to make sure they do the requisite homework on the topic and do not simply get up and say what is on their minds. I especially like the way he has both laid out his grading practices as well as his policy on academic dishonesty. Both of these are critical. Students should know the rule going in. If I had any suggestion here, I would underline or highlight comments such as the first sentence. Another thing I would suggest is that when he notes the assignments, he could include a sentence pointing out the key issue to be considered. It helps keep students' attention focused. "This week we will look at the key factors leading to state collapse in Rwanda," for example.

- *From a review of a course portfolio in English education:* The teaching projects reflect the work of an expert teacher, appropriate for one who prepares new teachers. . . . The variety of teaching techniques, such as student reading, class discussion, outside teaching, writing and verbal reports, taps into many learning styles. . . . This is not a random group of possible techniques, but a finite list. I interpret this to mean that she understands the benefits of each method and accordingly plans its use to achieve a certain end result . . . . I am continually struck by her detailed and student-centered approach to learning. . . . I believe [she], through her extensive and skilled use of teaching practices, not only provided the class with a thoughtful semester, but also gave them a model to use in their own teaching.

- *From a review of a course portfolio in construction management:* In my opinion, I perceive high quality teaching going on in the author's class. I am particularly impressed with his perspective on computer programs. I have long been an advocate of not teaching students a computer program without first teaching them the fundamentals. This is best done, from my perspective, by having the students first learn to do the same thing by hand. I use exactly the same methodology in my estimating course with good success. Once students learn the fundamentals properly, they are less likely to input an obviously false number or, even worse, rely upon an obviously false number generated by the computer. Computers are wonderful things, but used incorrectly they have a tendency to rob a student of the correct "sense" of what the answer should be.

Beyond affirming the general teaching techniques described in the portfolios, many reviewers focus on specific course projects and assignments, offering examples from their own courses and suggesting ways to better accomplish stated course goals via such projects and activities. In Exhibit 5.5,
the reviewer of a political science portfolio suggests that the structure of the
teacher's exams does not allow opportunities for students to demonstrate critical thinking about the course material. Other reviewers note places in portfolios where the representation of class time is not rendered in enough detail
for the review to make an adequate assessment about its value. The reviewer
of a nursing portfolio seeks more quantitative information about how student
contact time was organized to promote active learning, while the reviewer
of the communication studies portfolio suggests that linking the teacher's
goals to case study assignments would enhance the portfolio's organization
for documenting student learning.

Exhibit 5.5 Suggestions and Criticisms About Course Teaching Practices

- *From a review of a political science portfolio:* There appears to be a gap
  between the stated goals of the course and the structure of the exams. The instructor mentions that she wants students to move beyond
  the memorization of key terms and concepts and to think critically
  about international politics. The exams, however, are structured in a
  way that promotes the memorization of names, places, and events. The
  exams are basically short identification and answers. To be fair, the author includes concepts that require some explanation, but most of the
  material on the exam does not encourage students to think critically
  about world events or apply theories and concepts to international
  politics.

- *From a review of a course portfolio in nursing:* The author provides little
  quantitative information on the contact time spent in different educational activities in this course. Apparently, the predominant application
  of contact time is lecture on course content. If this is not true, the
  author needs to make that clearer in the portfolio. She does state that
  the student actor role-playing component of the course (which I like,
  see below) takes place 3–4 times a semester after major course

content. I would like to see an actual breakdown of the time spent lecturing versus any other in-class/contact time activity. . . . The opportunities to actively engage students in the material is also a bit difficult to evaluate from the information provided in the portfolio. During lectures on course content, did the author engage the students in dialogue or did she focus on transfer of information? From my own experience with pre-nursing, pre-medical, and pre-veterinary students, they can be a tough crowd in this respect (i.e., they would prefer to wait for the instructor to spoon-feed them the "facts" they need to function as medical professionals. They fail to realize—understandably—what an inadequate paradigm this is).

- *From a review of a communication studies portfolio:* The portfolio explains the case study assignments in some detail, reviewing how students responded to the cases during class. A connection between particular cases, the theories under consideration within the cases, and the specific learning goals for the respective cases would strengthen subsequent assessment of student learning. An electronic link or textual reference to specific case study assignments located in the appendix would also contribute to this section.

Quality of Student Understanding

Beyond describing a teacher's goals or pedagogical strategies, the essence of the course portfolio is in demonstrating the quality of student understanding. We all know of teachers who claim, "I'm a good teacher but my students don't learn." Ideally, good teaching is measured by the quality of student understanding, both for individual students but also in terms of the range of distribution for students within a class or across classes. A course portfolio also offers teachers an opportunity to analyze why student understanding might not be occurring at expected levels and to describe ongoing efforts to improve student performance. Thus this part of your review should focus on the teacher's assessment of the level and distribution of student learning in the highlighted activities and in the overall course. Common issues to discuss in a review include the following:

- Is student performance appropriate, in light of course goals, course level, and institution?

- Does student performance reflect challenging levels of conceptual understanding and critical evaluation of the material appropriate to the level of the course and of the students?

- Are the forms and methods of evaluation and assessment appropriate to the course?

- Are there multiple and diverse ways for students to demonstrate their understanding of and ability to use the ideas and content of the course?

- Is there an alignment between the weighting of course assignments in grade calculation with the relative importance of the course goals?

- Is there demonstration of an appropriate percentage of students who are achieving competence in the stated course goals, or identification of reasons why they might not be reaching these levels of competence?

- Are there suggested revisions or modifications to the course that could improve performance?

As discussed in Chapters 2 and 3, demonstrating the quality of student understanding is often the most difficult task for course portfolio authors. Consequently, reviewers of course portfolios often pinpoint ways that teachers could document and analyze their students' understanding more effectively, particularly in terms of tying assessments more explicitly to course goals. Exhibit 5.6 illustrates the types of issues and questions that reviewers commonly identify when they evaluate portfolios for evidence of student understanding. The construction management course reviewer, for instance, seeks more information regarding individual performance across multiple assignments as a way to compare team project grades to individual grades. The reviewers for both English and political science suggest that the writing assignments could be more demanding based on the quality of understanding represented in the sample student papers. In contrast, the reviewer of the communication studies portfolio focuses on ways that the teacher could better tie together her analysis of students' understanding with her assessment criteria. In this case, the problem is not the actual assignment or project but the way the teacher has documented and made visible excerpts of student understanding in relation to her stated criteria.

Exhibit 5.6 Review Excerpts Discussing the Quality of Student Understanding

- *From a review of a course portfolio in construction management:* All in all, I think the assessment area of his portfolio is the one area that could use some strengthening. For example, I expected to see some comparison of the examination results for his course, as it is my understanding that these are individual exams and may shed some light on an individual's learning. Additionally, the exams are 30% of the total course grade, the single highest component listed, which is bound to catch the student's interest. To a lesser extent, the same type of analysis could be done with the quizzes. It would be very interesting to see a comparison of test grades versus team grades for individual students, to test his hypothesis that some students were relying upon their teams to do the work. As an example, do your "C+" students score a "C+" on both the exams and the team project? Or do they score a "D" on the exam and an "A-" on the team project? Seeing this data on the graded components of the course would be enlightening and may help the author answer the question of who is really doing the work within each of the teams.

- *From a review of an English portfolio:* It's always difficult to assess how well students have learned. The portfolio author assessed their learning primarily through essay writing. Reviewing just three of those essays, I noted that students had found several of the concepts introduced in the course extremely helpful; their discussions of Gramsci's idea of the hegemony (as opposed to domination), for example, showed a clear understanding of this Marxist argument. Additionally student papers responded with facility to Louis Althusser's idea of the Ideological State Apparatus and a subject's interpellation. . . . Can the instructor be more demanding? While theory is difficult and the students can be expected to have many qualms about this area of study, their papers indicated they were capable of meeting the demands that emerged from the readings. There is a lot in the syllabus that shows what the instructor expects of himself, but less on what is expected of the students. It's reassuring but not demanding.

- *From a review of a political science portfolio:* I am concerned that some of this is a bit too much like high school and that it does not challenge students enough. A 13–15 page paper would appear to me to be more appropriate. Indeed, I would sacrifice one of the mid-terms to give them more time for the paper. I have the strong feeling that we often "dumb down" our courses rather than challenging students to be the "best and the brightest." I am bothered by the initial essay. This too, strikes me as more like high school than a university. Perhaps he covers this in some detail in his lectures, but I suspect that a good part of this is "student babble." They are not in a position to write a meaningful essay on this topic at this point in their education. I would either give them something on which to base such an essay or drop it. In fact, I think they would be better off to put more of their time on a mean-ingful term paper rather than the 5–7 page one noted in his syllabus.

- *From a review of a communication studies portfolio:* There is little specific annotated evidence from the two "very high" pass projects to sup-port this assessment. One must read each group's paper in light of the author's evaluative criteria to concur with the earlier assessment. If the portfolio included increased reflection on specific components and/or excerpts from each group project, the analysis of student learning might be further substantiated.

Evidence of Reflection and Development

Beyond representing student understanding within a course, the course port-folio is an opportunity for teachers to reflect upon their teaching in a sys-tematic and ongoing manner by identifying questions and issues that aid in future course development and improving teaching practices more generally. In this part of the review, then, your goal is to evaluate the teacher's reflec-tive consideration and development of the course. In other words, how does the teacher reflect on her overall teaching practices, course objectives, and promotion of student understanding? Questions you might consider include the following:

- Is there substantive reflection by the teacher on the achievement of course goals?

- Is there evidence of insightful analysis of teaching practice that resulted from consideration of student performance?

- Does the teacher identify meaningful relations between teaching practice and student performance?

• Docs the teacher provide evidence of changed teaching practice over successive course offerings in reaction to prior student understanding?

It is important to note that a successful course portfolio doesn't always showcase excellence in student understanding. Rather, some portfolios focus on identifying important questions to ask of one's teaching or on tracking developments in a course's design over several course offerings. Consequently, what a teacher's reflective consideration entails might significantly differ across course portfolios. Regardless of what a teacher's reflective consideration looks like, it is a central component of the portfolio that reviewers consider in their assessments. Exhibit 5.7 showcases several excerpts that illustrate how reviewers analyze and discuss a teacher's reflective development. The reviewer of the English portfolio appreciates the honest reflections of the teacher but suggests that this flexibility might hinder a more focused course design. The reviewer of the visual literacy portfolio comments on the effectiveness of the teacher's changes in assignments and grading rubrics and points to ways that this individual teacher's revisions might sponsor change throughout the visual literacy curriculum. The reviewer of the soil course portfolio responds warmly to the ethos that this portfolio projects regarding a teacher who cares greatly about student learning.

Exhibit 5.7 Review Excerpts Discussing Reflective Consideration and Development

---

• *From a review of a course portfolio in English:* In general, I appreciated the honest and sometimes tentative reflection that characterizes this portfolio. I also thought the language used to describe much of this instructor's teaching suggests a strong theme of spontaneity (what one might call the "by-the-seat-of-one's-pants" approach). In the teaching methods section, for instance, the instructor writes, "I don't plan [the techniques] out weeks ahead of time; rather, I choose the classroom method based on my sense of the room." Similarly, in the major writing projects section, the instructor explains, "I design these prompts . . . out of my sense of where the course has taken us to this point." I understand the thinking behind such remarks, and in many ways, it points to an admirable flexibility. Still, I think one's teaching should mostly be characterized—or at least represented—by deliberate planning, design, and implementation, all focused on one's teaching goals.

- *From a review of a course portfolio in visual literacy:* This entire portfolio is an obvious example of true reflection on both the project involvement and the benchmark portfolio. This instructor has made substantial changes to the course objectives, assignments, and evaluation methods based upon instructional reflection. The changes made by the instructor are positively reflected in the student comments, grades, and sample materials. I would expect that these improvements have also been noted by instructors of the complementary and upper-level coursework involving these students. Continued follow-up with these students would provide useful material for continued reflection and course development. Finally, as previously mentioned, it would appear to be useful for this instructor to collaboratively develop a curriculum portfolio with the other instructors in the visual literacy curriculum. This would provide the opportunity for reflection on how individual component changes are impacting the curriculum and vice versa.

- *From a review of a field science soil course:* He shows a tremendous concern for the students. He wants them to achieve and has developed the practices needed for them to achieve. He also is processing how these practices are working for achieving the goals. He is willing to allow students to go back and try again, and he himself is willing to go back and change an activity if it was not working. He has changed the course to better reflect his teaching style and I imagine that it will continue to change as he becomes more confident in his abilities to work with and motivate students.

Reviewers' Teaching Experience

The last category does not focus on the portfolio but rather on your own expertise as a reviewer. This component of your review should offer insight into your background and qualifications. This information is especially important if the review is going to be used for summative purposes, such as a promotion and tenure review. This section allows you to establish your ethos as a reviewer, to demonstrate that you are qualified to render an opinion regarding teaching practices, course design, and course content. Beyond these factors, it is also useful to discuss your own teaching context so that potential readers of the review can better understand the perspective you are bringing to the review process. You might discuss some of the following questions:

- What similar courses have you taught (e.g., class size, level, content)?

- Have you taught using a similar format (e.g., course structure, presentation format)?

- Are there particular values/attitudes you bring to particular pedagogical strategies and approaches or course goals?

- How long have you been teaching? What is your typical teaching load and/or responsibilities at your institution?

The excerpts in Exhibit 5.8 show a range of ways that reviewers establish their credibility in writing reviews. The first two reviews (both for a political science course) illustrate how the first reviewer describes disciplinary expertise while the second has taught a similar type of elective course but not within the discipline of political science. The reviewer from English describes her experiences in teaching the same course content for two different course sizes. In contrast, the reviewers of the visual literacy and nursing portfolios note that while they come from different disciplinary backgrounds, they share similar goals with respect to teaching basic skill sets and active learning strategies. The reviewer of the nursing portfolio shows an especially high interest in the author's pedagogical goals because they are similar to her own. The reviewer of the philosophy course portfolio notes shared challenges that he and the portfolio author face while also noting different institutional pressures (such as class size) that might shape their teaching strategies.

Exhibit 5.8 Excerpts From Reviewers on Their Teaching Experiences

- *From a review of a course portfolio from political science:* I have taught numerous courses in comparative as well as international relations. I have used similar approaches including guest speakers, simulations, midterms, finals, and research papers. The classes have normally contained about 20 students.

- *From a review of a course portfolio from political science:* I have taught numerous courses although my content area is different from this course. I also teach a course that is an elective that stands alone in the departmental curricula. It is a constant challenge to ensure the relevancy of the course. Because of this, I try to make the course fun with a high likelihood for success. I try to focus more on in-class and out-of-class activities that help the students make a stronger connection between the course and their lives.

- *From a review of a course portfolio from English:* I have taught classes similar to this one for more than 20 years. While I have taught this course in small sections, currently I offer it only in large sections. I have taught this class in nearly the same way as the author with about the same results. I, too, hope to transform my class into a more assignment-centered course that allows students to learn something that they will retain beyond the moment they finish the exams.

- *From a review of a course portfolio from visual literacy:* My teaching experience is in journalism coursework that focuses on the same type of basic skill development. I am also the primary instructor for an upper-level course that incorporated all of the basic skills. Therefore, I understand the need to break down skills and assist students in the mastery of those skills to enhance their experience in the upper-level courses. I also appreciate the ability to really challenge students in the upper-level courses because I know they have mastered the necessary basic skill sets. Our courses incorporate a series of assignments that reinforce basic skills while incorporating new or advanced skills each week.

- *From a review of a course portfolio from nursing:* I have taught physiology to undergraduates, graduate students and medical and veterinary medical students. While I have never taught in a nursing program, I am intimately aware of the underlying physiology, pharmacology, anatomy, biochemistry that a nursing student would need to master in order to effectively understand pathology and treatment. More importantly, I do have considerable personal experience with a mode of "active learning" applied to (in this case) undergraduate bioengineering students. In that team-taught (two-instructor) course, we required our students to work in teams on the design of novel prosthetics. The groups worked on competing designs and submitted a written outline and gave an oral presentation. These oral presentations were analogous (although not identical) to the student actor scenarios of the author. They certainly pressurized the students a bit and forced them to perform in public in a way that few of them had experienced before. The projects as a whole also provided these students with a mock real-world experience such as they will find in their careers in the biotechnology industry (again analogous to the mock real-world nursing scenarios of the author). This experience of mine is the driving force behind my interest and enthusiasm for the author's goal to institute active learning in her course.

• *From a review of a course portfolio from philosophy:* Having taught philosophy courses at a Catholic liberal arts college over the past five years, I share many of the author's concerns. The primary difference between my teaching experiences and his is undoubtedly the institutional context of class. I do not (nor have I ever) taught in a large lecture hall, nor do we break the class into Friday discussion groups led by TAs at my university. Classes are smaller (maximum of 25) and the students take Introduction to Philosophy because it is part of the core curriculum. Of the teaching practices that he has evolved, the ones I can relate to most directly are those that concern the clarification of high expectations and rendering difficult concepts more accessible.

What's Next?

This chapter explored the issues and questions involved in seeking a critical review and evaluation of your course portfolio. In the next chapter we describe how collaborative efforts to document and assess teaching and students' learning benefits individual faculty members, programs, and campuses.

6 Using Course Portfolios to Foster Campus Collaboration

Another very important component of peer review associated with the course portfolio is the collaboration and community building that occurs among faculty as they write their portfolios. Beyond valuing the finished product of the course portfolio, faculty often note the importance of the collaborative process as central to their learning about their teaching. In addition, this collaboration, whether it be with peers at the department level or with faculty across a campus, plays an essential role in developing an overall campus climate supportive of teaching excellence.

In fact, collaboration with other teachers is a vital part of writing a course portfolio. It is possible, of course, to write a course portfolio in isolation, but most of us rely on at least one other person for support, encouragement, and critical input as we think through our course goals, describe our teaching practices, and evaluate student learning. Collaboration with colleagues can give us new perspectives on our own teaching as well. Often we focus on the minutiae of a particular course or instructional strategy (how to use small groups more effectively or how to develop a grading rubric) without considering broader pedagogical issues (how a particular course's objectives meet the overarching goals of a curriculum or whether a particular assignment is representative of student learning expected more generally). It is much easier to focus on the ratio of lecture to discussion than to question structural issues in a major or the relationship of various courses to the general education curriculum. Discussions with colleagues help encourage thinking about these larger issues and lead ultimately to more conscious decisions regarding our own teaching.

This chapter discusses the important role played by disciplinary colleagues and by faculty from other departments and colleges as one type of peer review. It gives several examples of collaboration between peers at various levels, showing how faculty have used the process of writing course portfolios to strengthen coordination between those teaching within the same department or in related disciplines and to share teaching techniques and insights across disciplines. It also provides examples of how faculty collaboration through peer review has supported teaching improvement and teaching excellence more generally at our institution. Finally, it gives some practical suggestions for how to initiate and sustain productive discussions about teaching and learning with your peers on campus.

Collaboration Within Departments

The most basic type of collaboration in writing a course portfolio involves working with a partner or a small group of colleagues from your own department or from a closely related discipline. Having another person to whom you are accountable as you work on your portfolio provides each of you with additional motivation to stay with the process, especially if you are faced with multiple demands on your time. More importantly, a peer from your discipline, even if his or her research differs from yours, is best placed to appreciate the specific challenges and issues that arise from teaching within your field as well as those posed by the students who take those courses.

Your conversations may be informal: They might occur in brief exchanges as you pass by each other's offices or involve getting together over lunch to talk about your target course. But it is also helpful to have a more formal structure for discussion and specific feedback as you write each of the memos for your course portfolio. These conversations can also be extended to the departmental level, if several of you are working on course portfolios. We have found that there tends to be an inverse relationship between the number of people working together to produce course portfolios and the degree of structure and formality in meetings, as well as to the time required to meet. If you and one or two others from your department are each writing a course portfolio, you can exchange memos and discuss your teaching on a relatively informal basis. If four or more people are involved in the process, it is generally a good idea to collaborate on two levels—each person works closely with a partner, and, as schedules permit, several people meet more formally to talk as a group about course portfolios and curricular issues more generally. Another alternative is for participants in disciplinary teams to share materials and post comments via email or an electronic workspace organized through an online course management system (e.g., Blackboard). Typically these electronic forums work well for larger teams, when it can be difficult to schedule a meeting that everyone can attend.

Peer collaboration at the department level can be structured in various ways: It can focus on one course that is or has been taught by two or more individuals; it can look at two courses taught in sequence; or it can involve larger questions of curricular planning, such as courses required for majors or for the general education curriculum. In each case, writing a course portfolio can be a springboard to further discussion about individual teaching practices and larger issues relevant to the discipline. For example, a professor in agronomy and horticulture wrote a benchmark portfolio for his class on soil resources in order to update instruction in a course whose basic parameters had been set more than 15 years earlier by a previous teacher. His thinking about the course was aided by the fact that his departmental collaborator not only taught the course herself but was also writing a benchmark portfolio for a course for which his class was a prerequisite. His portfolio partner was thus familiar with the problems and constraints that he faced in revising his course, and she could act as a sounding board as he discussed each of his memos with her. Their regular conversations contributed significantly to their process of writing a course portfolio and to broader conversations about how to improve their students' learning:

> Weekly discussions of teaching method, content, and effectiveness provided us an outlet to share our experiences and our perceptions of what was and was not working in the classroom. Each meeting was a lesson critique of what we had just finished teaching that week, while the experience and our perceptions of student learning were still fresh in our minds. These sessions enabled

us to assess whether or not we were teaching to our goals for the class, and to brainstorm on alternative methods of presenting the material. We were always searching for ways to incorporate active learning methods into the course as much as possible.

Similarly, two professors in advertising taught the fourth and fifth courses in a six-course sequence required of all advertising majors. As one of the partners explained, they had clear objectives for their involvement in peer review:

> We wanted to use our portfolios to generate discussion in our sequence in order to strengthen the core of our program and to link goals so that students would be better prepared for the next course in the curriculum. It would also allow us to position our advertising curriculum as a strong strategic program in journalism and mass communication education. In the past, there had been inconsistencies in learning outcomes in the two courses. Several sections of the courses had been taught by adjunct professors who focused on different goals that did not necessarily "link" the two courses to fit into the bigger picture. We had talked about how to improve the courses prior to participating in the peer review project, but writing and discussing the three interactions really helped us focus on goals that had been set forth by our accrediting body. We were both able to change specific assignments to focus on these goals and improve student learning. The process helped us to see how the two courses focused on similar goals using different teaching techniques. After completing our two course portfolios we were able to focus on one of those goals (to develop critical and independent thinking) and wrote a scholarly paper about how that goal can be achieved in two core courses in an advertising program using the peer review of teaching project.

As this account suggests, the curricular impact of a course portfolio is heightened when several members of a department write their own portfolios at the same time. Other faculty members have noted that the conversations they had while working on their portfolios helped them see how their target course fit into the curriculum and gave them a better idea of how courses were linked within the department. One way to focus such discussions is by emphasizing key concepts within the discipline. For example, a professor of anthropology and geography characterized the meetings of her department peers as providing "useful discussion of how the concept of kinship is linked through the curriculum, discussed down the line." A professor of English described the practical impact of these discussions in her department:

> I was teaching the introduction to English studies and [my port-folio partner] was teaching introduction to literary and critical theory, and we shared some students in those courses. Talking about the students we shared and the goals we had for our courses . . . was a really nice opportunity for me to learn more about the curriculum, about the students, and their experience with that curriculum.

While any conversation with peers can be valuable for thinking differently about one's teaching, structured discussions of specific questions that you are all currently addressing have particular value. Faculty who have participated in the Peer Review of Teaching Project at the University of Nebraska–Lincoln have highlighted the value of conversations with departmental partners as they are in the process of writing the three memos designed to generate a portfolio. As a professor of family and consumer science said:

> Discussing with my colleague and reviewing her syllabus vali-dated what I have been doing and also taught me how I could make improvements in my syllabus and my teaching. It forced me to think more in depth about my class and why I do things the way I do.

A professor of accounting found that "the idea that we could share what works and what didn't work in our classes was incredibly helpful." Like many teachers, a professor of political science commented on the mutual support that came from discussing his teaching: "It's nice to know that some of your colleagues are struggling with the same things that you're struggling with. And it's always good to hear what they're doing in class to energize their students."

Structuring the Conversations

A good way to guide the conversations of disciplinary partners or a team is to structure them around three key interactions, corresponding to the three benchmark memos discussed in Chapter 2, focused on course goals, classroom activities, and student learning. In each of these interactions, the peer discussion expands beyond the contents of the memo to identify links between student performance, course objectives, and the broader curriculum. Exhibit 6.1 outlines a general procedure for these discussions. Each interaction has four steps, which the participants would repeat for each of the three memos.

Memo 1. One of the goals for the discussion of the first memo is to identify shared objectives for student learning and to relate them to the broader departmental or college curriculum. You may also want to identify promising outcomes that your department team would like to focus on as part of your peer review of teaching project, such as a deeper understanding of what others teach, greater familiarity with different courses and how they interrelate, or the introduction of different teaching approaches.

Memo 2. As part of the conversation on the second memo, we encourage peer collaborators not only to exchange their memos with their department team partner but also to invite their partner to visit the target class. The focus of this visit should be on learning from one another about teaching approaches and practices rather than on evaluating each other. This peer observation may provide useful insight to both partners, through discussion about teaching practices or feedback about use of time in class. As a result of visits to each other's classroom, each partner should have a better understanding of what takes place during class sessions.

Before each visit, the partners should meet to discuss what the teacher would like the observer to focus on while in the classroom. This allows the teacher to outline his or her goals for the upcoming session, express specific concerns or questions he or she might have, and describe the types of feedback

Exhibit 6.1 Procedure for Interaction With Departmental Peers

Interaction Part	Activity	Description
I	Individual preparation for interaction	Write benchmark memo.
II	Interaction with department team partner	Department team partners share their memos and their course syllabus.
III	Discussion with department team partner	Team partners should have a conversation focusing on two main areas: 1) The interaction: What were some of the key insights each participant gained as a result of writing the memo? What insights resulted from reading a team partner's memo? 2) The contents of each memo: How do your course goals, classroom procedures, and the resultant student learning relate to departmental priorities? To the broader departmental or area curriculum?
IV	Follow-up on interaction	Following the discussion with your partner, review your benchmark memo and (if appropriate) add one to two pages on "what I have learned" (e.g., potential changes you will make, new ideas, additional thoughts) as a result of writing the interaction and meeting with your partner.

he or she would like from the observer. For instance, it is often hard to gauge how much of a class period is spent on different types of instruction, whether lecturing, discussion, question and answer, or group work. An observer can provide a more objective sense of what proportion of the class was spent on each activity, especially if he or she is asked beforehand to keep track of time in this way. Likewise, if a partner explains to the peer collaborator what points are most important for the students to understand and be able to explain, he or she can give much more specific feedback about the discussions of small groups in the classroom. Or the teacher may want to experiment with a new teaching technique and would like the observer to focus particularly on how students react to it.

After the visit, team partners should have an informal conversation about the classroom visits. What did each of you learn about your own teaching, whether from the feedback of your team partner or from observation of your partner's class? By using this approach, classroom visits are transformed from an "evaluative" moment into an opportunity for growth and mutual discovery.

Memo 3. Instructors may not be able to finish the third memo until the semester has ended. Still, it is possible to begin a rough draft, listing potential ways of documenting student learning, and then discussing your ideas with the team partners. Because they also have to assess and evaluate student learning in your discipline, departmental peers can be especially helpful in brainstorming about ways to present student learning to others. As with the previous interactions, this conversation should move from specific questions about how each colleague evaluates student learning in the course to broader departmental issues. For instance, how can student performance on individual course assignments be used to assess student learning across a curriculum? As a part of this conversation, the partners or team might also want to include a discussion of other ways to evaluate teaching. Given the discussions on the first two memos, what other options exist to evaluate teaching in the department? What combination of student performance and these other options would offer a more complete picture of the students' experiences in each course?

Peer Review of Common or Team-Taught Courses

The discussions prompted by exchange of the three memos can be particularly useful when faculty members from different departments are involved in a common program or a team-taught course. For instance, the visual literacy program at the University of Nebraska–Lincoln requires its students to take a yearlong course taught in four modules by eight or nine faculty drawn from three different colleges: the Hixon-Lied College of Fine and Performing Arts, the College of Architecture, and the College of Human Resources and Family Sciences. The 250 students who take the course each year rotate from one module and instructor to another in no fixed sequence. Thus the background of students taking a module later in the sequence is quite different from that of the students who took the module as the first in their sequence, and this creates a number of pedagogical challenges for the instructors involved. Writing a course portfolio for their own modules and discussing their interactions helps them to coordinate and refine their teaching across the various modules.

A professor of textiles, clothing, and design described the group and one-on-one discussions that the visual literacy team engaged in over the course of the year's involvement in the process as:

> the single most important factor in the exercise. Individual reflection was important, but the nitty-gritty carving away at the issues that were most pertinent to our area, the work of these ongoing discussions, was really key in helping me to define what it was I needed to focus and work on, what objectives/outcomes I wanted to envision for myself, and whether or not I was approaching them. Because the four of us were fully engaged in the visual literacy program at the time, and because it's such an intensive cluster of courses, we quickly developed a really dynamic synergy among ourselves. People were unfailingly generous in the feedback exchanged during the year, and that generosity stemmed from an understanding that not only would each of us benefit individually from the work, but that the academic program in which we were/are investing so much of ourselves as educators would also benefit. That's exactly what happened.

A professor of art and art history concurred about the importance of these peer conversations and pointed to the significant course revisions that resulted:

> The benchmark portfolio discussions with my visual literacy colleagues gave structure and specific goals to our already frequent chats about our courses within the program. We often shared ideas for solving classroom challenges, whether they were for learning students' names quickly, maintaining a rigorous studio atmosphere or developing new assignments. The most specific and useful result of our discussions must be the development of our individual grading rubrics. Informed by the assigned readings, we compared strategies, formats, philosophies, etc. and developed rubrics that were tied to our course goals and assignments. Implementing these rubrics increased the rigor of our studios, helped students understand how we evaluate work *and* saved us time in grading. The full-time faculty members in the visual literacy program continue to have a strong dialog that always includes references to our peer review of teaching experiences.

The professor of textiles, clothing, and design described the changes that had resulted to his own teaching:

> My experience in the peer review process has helped me to clarify my own expectations of student performance and has helped me to convey more clearly to the students what each project exploration entails and what they should be looking for and working toward as they give form to the respective concepts.
>
> The fallout from our team experience has had an impact throughout the program as we've shared much of what we learned with our visual literacy colleagues, and the insights that we gained fed in numerous ways into the eventual adjustments and changes that we've effected in the visual literacy program since that year.

While it is most common for faculty from the same department or from related disciplines to engage in these focused discussions of their benchmark memos, it is also possible to form a group on the basis of similar pedagogical challenges or approaches to teaching. For example, a group of faculty from three departments (educational administration, agricultural leadership and communication, and special education and communication disorders) who were all teaching classes using distance learning found exchanging and discussing their memos to be very beneficial, for it enabled them to share tips and techniques about how to use the Internet for instruction. A professor of educational administration described both the structure and the impact of their interactions:

> What was unique about our group was the common interest all four of us had in teaching distance-learning students. We all had experience in teaching students at a distance, but we were very interested in learning from each other what we might do to improve our teaching and our students' learning. During the academic year we shared ideas of strategies that we believed were successful in our teaching and discussed areas where we needed to improve. Our numerous discussions contained insights that enabled all of us to profit from this experience. Each of us spent many hours reading materials we prepared, reacting to ideas that we posted on our discussion forum, and working on a course portfolio. At no time in my 34-year career here had I focused so intently on my teaching. The experience was definitely a highlight for me. Students in classes I have taught since this experience are the true beneficiaries. Materials that I share with students are better organized, assignments are more focused, assessments are better linked to the objectives of the class and students [are] more satisfied with their experiences in the distance classes I teach. All of my colleagues shared the same enthusiasm I had for the peer review project and all commented that they acquired a significant amount of new information from our interactions.

Collaboration Across Campus

This professor's experience demonstrates the value of faculty conversations that cross departmental or program lines. Mutual support and new ideas about teaching are not limited to our disciplinary colleagues or to those teaching similar courses. It can be valuable to meet regularly with faculty from other departments and colleges to discuss what you are learning as you write your course portfolio and to brainstorm about ways to encourage and evaluate student learning. By extending beyond the concerns of a particular department or college, these conversations encourage reflection on similar issues that teachers face across campus and a recognition that a question one particular teacher may face is often representative of a larger issue that others are dealing with as well. As Hutchings (1993) asserts, "There's a growing recognition that what's really needed to improve teaching is a campus culture in which good practice can thrive, one where teachers talk together about teaching, inquire into its effects, and take collective responsibility for its quality" (p. v).

Conversations with faculty from other departments and colleges can be an eye-opening experience, revealing differences in types of goals, approaches to learning, and student audiences. Specific disciplinary requirements can lead to very different methods of teaching and evaluation of learning. As we listen to the issues and challenges of those from different disciplines, we may identify with a professor of English who said, "I often walked away from those conversations feeling like, 'Boy, we teach in different worlds.'" But these differences can also help us approach our own discipline from a new angle. A professor in construction management pointed to the advantages of such cross-fertilization:

> These are really creative people from textiles, and English, and various other departments, which I personally find very helpful . . . I've been trained in engineering and I know the logical path, and that's why this kind of environment really helps me expand.

A professor of history noted the new perspective that came from listening to colleagues teaching first-semester calculus wrestle with the problem of ensuring both deep understanding and coverage of the required content so that students would be ready for the second-semester course:

> I was always frustrated with the amount of material I was expected to cover in my one-semester world history course. But after I saw the challenges they faced in making sure their students finished the required number of chapters *and* understood all of the concepts, I began to appreciate the tremendous freedom I have to select the topics and the emphases within my course and to determine the appropriate trade-off between deep understanding and content coverage.

Beyond these broader issues of perspective, we should not let the differences between disciplines blind us to the common issues that confront teachers and that stimulate the exchange of new ideas and techniques. An advertising professor noted that "it was interesting to see that many of us run into the same problems/issues/roadblocks, no matter what discipline we're in." A professor of political science added, "It's just helpful sharing with colleagues regarding what they're doing, talking more and thinking more consciously about what you're doing in the classroom from A to Z." A professor of industrial engineering elaborated on the benefits of these conversations, expressing a common reaction of peer review participants at the end of the project:

> While developing the course portfolio has been invaluable for me to critically review my course, I was surprised to realize that the focused discussions with other project participants have had the biggest impact on me. Whether one is teaching a large lecture in engineering, economics, or psychology, there are similar teaching and student learning issues in terms of classroom management, presentation of materials, and student assessment. Due to the nature of the peer review project, we were able to share our issues, offer suggestions, and explore best practices among academic disciplines that would rarely interact.

As a professor of accounting summed up, "Colleagues are colleagues, and I learned from colleagues engaged in teaching, whether it's in my department or across the university."

One important difference between cross-campus collaboration and the conversations that take place with departmental colleagues is the degree of structure necessary for the former. Because more people are generally involved in the cross-campus meetings, they can be much harder to schedule once the semester begins. When working with a large number of faculty with varying schedules, it is generally best to set dates and times for all the meetings at the beginning of the semester. With advance notice like this, participants can reserve the necessary time for the meetings before their own calendars are filled.

Readings and Resources for Departmental and Campus Collaboration

Conversations at these large group meetings can be more productive if they are based on one or more essays, articles, or book chapters that everyone has read beforehand. We have found it helpful to assemble and distribute to each faculty participant a notebook containing all the materials, articles, and examples we will address over the entire year. We also provide each participant with a set of teaching-related books to support them as they write their course portfolios. These readings are useful for presenting larger issues and concepts related to teaching and learning. A set of common readings ensures that all the faculty working on course portfolios have a shared level of knowledge, so that no one needs to feel excluded from the discussion because of lack of background. It also contributes to the creation of a common vocabulary about teaching, learning, and assessment, which can in turn be used in the support and promotion of teaching excellence on a campus level, such as the evaluation of candidate files for tenure or promotion or for teaching awards.

Each memo and peer interaction raises different types of questions, and so for our discussions we use a broad variety of readings, from the theoretical and abstract to the practical and concrete. The readings may be related to a general pedagogical issue, a specific teaching practice, or some aspect of portfolio development. As faculty begin the process of writing a course portfolio, for instance, they might benefit from readings introducing them to the goals and philosophy of the scholarship of teaching and learning. A short introduction to the scholarship of teaching, such as a section of Glassick, Huber, and Maeroff's (1997) *Scholarship Assessed* or Bass's (1999) "The Scholarship of Teaching: What's the Problem?" can generate discussion that helps individuals look beyond the course portfolio as a simple description of their course and see it as a tool for deeper inquiry into the intellectual work of teaching. Because we have often become used to teaching in isolation, many faculty are unaware of the larger issues related to the scholarship of teaching. Discussions of these broader issues help instructors to position their work within a larger conversation and to understand that they can approach their teaching in the same way that they approach their research.

When preparing to write the first benchmark memo, many faculty find it particularly helpful to be given readings that address issues of course design. Most of us received little training in graduate school on how to organize and develop curriculum and learning objectives, and so we appreciate being introduced to the principles and practices developed by education specialists. Participants in our program have benefited from exposure to concepts such as Wiggins and McTighe's (2001) backward design or to Walvoord and Anderson's (1998) view that effective grading begins with setting measurable goals for learning. Fink's (2003) suggestions about how to design significant learning experiences is another starting point for stimulating discussion among faculty.

Because of the tremendous diversity of teaching situations across campus, a smorgasbord approach, presenting a wide range of options concerning classroom practices, often works best when selecting readings for discussion in conjunction with the second memo. Faculty often appreciate resources such as *McKeachie's Teaching Tips* (2001) or Davis's *Tools for Teaching* (1993), which contain many practical suggestions for everything from preparing a syllabus to how to use the last day of class. Similarly, Angelo and Cross's (1993) *Classroom Assessment Techniques* describes a variety of measures to assess different types of student learning over the course of the semester. No matter what their background or particular pedagogical concerns, teachers almost always find something in these books that applies to their particular classroom experience.

As they work on the third memo, faculty often find it helpful to look at a variety of course portfolios, whether from similar or quite different disciplines. We thus refer them to our Peer Review of Teaching web site (www.courseportfolio.org), which has more than 200 portfolios describing courses ranging from the introductory to the graduate level in a wide range of disciplines. These examples can give new ideas about the many ways to demonstrate student learning. Some faculty have found it helpful to write an external review of another portfolio, because it gives them ideas about what they might want to include in their own portfolio or how they can present their assessments of student learning in their own classroom.

Of course, numerous other materials help promote discussion on teaching. Journals devoted to teaching issues, such as *Change, College Teaching,* or *The American Educator,* are a valuable source of articles for discussion. Disciplinary journals that focus on teaching or collections of essays on teaching within a particular discipline may contain articles that are the basis for discussions among departmental partners or teams, and some of these readings may be broad enough that their suggestions—for instance, on how to lead discussions more effectively—are helpful for faculty in several different disciplines. A group of faculty from the same department may decide to include discussion of a book related to teaching within their discipline as part of their regular meetings. For example, historians may find the essays collected in Stearns, Seixas, and Wineburg's (2000) *Knowing, Teaching, and Learning History* particularly helpful as they discuss the broad range of classes that make up the history curriculum, while the research of educational psychologist Sam Wineburg (2001), presented in *Historical Thinking and Other Unnatural Acts,* could prompt lively discussion on a more theoretical level.

Many campuses have their own statements or policies concerning what constitutes outstanding and effective teaching, and these documents are especially important for faculty to discuss in relation to improving the campus culture for teaching. As a part of the Peer Review of Teaching Project at the University of Nebraska–Lincoln, faculty regularly discuss the framework for representing teaching written by our Academy of Distinguished Teachers, which in turn has helped increase familiarity with and support for the criteria outlined in the document. Campus centers for teaching and learning are a valuable resource for help in identifying readings appropriate to your particular interests and needs. Choices for reading are therefore best determined by your specific campus culture and situation.

While a set of common readings helps unite faculty from different disciplines in their discussions about teaching, other materials can foster fruitful exchange of ideas about teaching. As the statements quoted earlier in this section suggest, we often learn from others as they describe their own teaching experiences and share examples of student work from their classes. For instance, instructors might be asked to bring one example of student work that raises a problem or concern for them as teachers. Faculty who use group work might be asked to bring one example of assessment that they use to evaluate group work. Or teachers who use multiple-choice exams could each bring a copy of an exam and then collectively analyze and discuss the ratio of rote memorization to higher-order thinking represented in the questions. Such teaching artifacts often generate lively discussions as faculty develop a much richer understanding of what goes on in their colleagues' classrooms.

Organizing the Campus Conversation

Depending on the size of the group, these conversations about teaching practices may involve everyone, or you may want to break into smaller groups of four or five people to discuss general teaching questions. Exhibit 6.2 lists sample questions that are useful for starting conversations about teaching.

Exhibit 6.2 Teaching Questions

General questions

1) What are different approaches for teaching?

2) How does one measure student learning?

3) What can we expect from our students?

4) How does one document teaching efforts?

5) What is the right balance among student and peer voices in the evaluation of teaching?

6) How does one use student assessments to guide and improve course instruction and content?

7) To what extent should our expectations of new faculty, mid-career faculty, and veteran faculty differ with regard to teaching methods, student satisfaction, and teaching effectiveness?

8) If you could give the provost one idea for supporting/improving teaching at this campus, what would it be?

Questions on teaching strategies

1) What is one successful strategy you use for learning student names?

2) What is one successful strategy you use for managing classroom disruptions (e.g., students late to class, reading newspapers, cell phones ringing)?

3) What is one successful strategy you use for checking if students comprehended material in a given class session?

4) What is one successful strategy you use for ensuring students turn in work on time?

5) What is one successful strategy you use for managing student papers (collecting, returning)?

6) What is one successful strategy you use for managing student groups?

Questions on student motivation

1) As a professor, are student grades in your courses a reflection of what they have learned?

2) Given the diversity of students (academic preparedness, emotional preparedness), how do you teach classes to this range?

Questions on impact of technology on teaching

1) How has the use of technology changed how you teach?

2) How has technology affected how your students learn?

3) How do you see teaching changing in the next 10 years?

In addition to this more general discussion of teaching, faculty usually appreciate having time during these large meetings to discuss their progress on the memos they are writing. Exhibit 6.3 gives some typical questions related to the benchmark memos and to creating the portfolio that can be used to initiate discussions.

Exhibit 6.3 Questions on Benchmark Interactions

Benchmark Memo 1 (course goals)

1) What are your course goals?

2) Why are these goals important?

3) What do you want students coming out of your course to know or to be able to do?

4) What issues do you want to investigate in your teaching?

5) What do you hope to learn from your participation?

6) How do you plan to use your portfolio?

Benchmark Memo 2 (classroom activities)

1) How are your assignments connected to the goals of the course?

2) What course activities (e.g., exams, homework, discussion) work best? What data/evidence do you have to show that they worked? Which would you change?

3) Would you change the class structure?

4) Is there a meaningful relationship between your teaching practices and student performance?

Benchmark Memo 3 (measuring student learning)

1) What does students' work so far tell you about how well they understand the ideas that are central to the course?

2) So far, how well has student work met your intellectual goals for the course?

3) Has the distribution of achievement by students been up to your expectations?

4) Has it been comparable to previous offerings of the same course?

5) What types of data you are collecting from your course? How do you envision summarizing this data and presenting it to a reader of your portfolio?

6) Share one example of student work from your course. Using that example:

   • Explain what the example shows (and does not show) about student learning in your course.

- Explain what else you might look for in your course to give further information on learning.

- Do others agree that your example demonstrates to them what you think it does?

Developing the benchmark course portfolio

1) What course goals do you think you met?

2) How do you know your course goals were met? What data or evidence do you have to represent that your course goals were met?

3) Which goals did you not meet?

4) What goals you change the next time you teach this course?

5) What goals will you better emphasize or support the next time you teach the course?

6) Has the process of reviewing your course and writing a portfolio been useful to you? In what ways?

7) What question(s) about your teaching have you found interesting to investigate?

8) Did you learn new ideas about teaching and learning through your writing?

9) What have you learned about yourself as a teacher from writing a course portfolio?

Although faculty become involved with the peer review process in order to produce a course portfolio, many find, at the end of the process, that their involvement in these larger conversations about teaching has had the greatest impact on them. A professor of agronomy expressed a view held by many of our participants:

> The most beneficial aspect of the project was the opportunity to meet other university faculty to share and discuss undergraduate teaching experiences. The discussion groups and reading selections provided a forum for sharing among colleagues that yielded many useful teaching tips, common stumbling blocks and unique solutions, and the chance to get a glimpse into the teaching

experience of faculty in diverse disciplines. This personal contact was a highlight of the review process.

Promoting Teaching Excellence on Campus

One frequent outcome of cross-disciplinary faculty discussions is enthusiasm for raising the visibility of teaching more generally. A common lament on many campuses is that teaching is not valued as much as research, and faculty may feel that they can do little by themselves to effect significant change. Writing a course portfolio and talking about issues of teaching and student learning often prompts individual faculty members to play a greater role in encouraging broader teaching initiatives across campus.

In fact, discussions about teaching with like-minded colleagues can be habit-forming, causing faculty to seek out more opportunities for such exchanges and so heightening awareness of teaching issues on campus. A survey of faculty who have been through the Peer Review of Teaching Project at the University of Nebraska-Lincoln showed that 70% feel they have become more connected with the group of faculty who create and advocate campus-wide teaching policies, and more than one-half said their experience has helped them develop leadership skills in supporting and improving teaching at the campus level. The respondents have taken part in teaching initiatives at every level, from encouraging regular brown-bag lunch meetings to discuss teaching within their departments to serving on committees that select recipients of campus-wide teaching awards. A number of faculty members created a task force to improve the student retention rate, and the task force in turn sponsored efforts to improve teaching of the general education classes taken by freshmen. As a professor of anthropology noted:

> The values of the Peer Review of Teaching Project have dominated the efforts of that group. I think we've changed from a simple view of "keep the kids" to "how can we create an environment that will make students want to stay?"

Other individuals have become more involved in the program to support new and untenured faculty, lead workshops on teaching-related issues, or serve on the Teaching Council, which oversees and coordinates teaching initiatives on campus.

Faculty who have written a course portfolio describing the intellectual work of their own teaching feel more confident about evaluating and critiquing the teaching of others, whether they do this as external reviewers of a course portfolio, as part of the promotion and tenure process, or as members of a committee evaluating nominations for teaching awards. Three-quarters of our respondents agreed that their participation in peer review had helped them build a vocabulary for discussing and evaluating teaching, and almost 90% felt that they had developed a better sense of what constitutes an effective course portfolio.

Individuals who have reflected seriously on their own teaching through the process of peer review can function more effectively as teaching mentors to graduate students and new faculty. Some may wish to continue their involvement in peer review by assuming leadership responsibilities for a formal peer review program on campus. For example, all the faculty leaders of peer review projects at our five-campus consortium began their involvement with writing a benchmark portfolio for one of their courses. Others may wish to continue the scholarly investigation of their own teaching by writing an inquiry course portfolio or by facilitating a small group of faculty who are writing inquiry portfolios. Whatever individual faculty choose to do after they have written a course portfolio, almost all of them agree that writing a course portfolio, in collaboration with departmental and campus colleagues, has made them better teachers and increased their involvement in initiatives to improve teaching.

What's Next

We have considered a range of ways in which peers can collaborate in the process of writing a course portfolio, from informal conversations with a departmental partner to more structured meetings that bring together teachers from all parts of the campus. You may be convinced that such discussions are beneficial, but you aren't certain how to go about encouraging such collaboration. Chapter 7 addresses the practical and logistical issues that arise in setting up a peer review program to support the writing of course portfolios and encourage greater collaboration among teachers.

7 Creating a Campus Community for the Peer Review of Teaching

While the previous chapters have focused on how you can explore, document, and share the effectiveness of your teaching, the objective of this chapter is to provide insight into starting a campus peer review of teaching program. Based on the successful campus model we have developed over 10 years, and those of our project consortium partners (Indiana University–Bloomington, Kansas State University, Texas A&M, University of Kansas, and University of Michigan), this chapter offers suggestions for creating a campus peer review program designed to promote the intellectual work of teaching and to support a campus's efforts for achieving teaching excellence. We offer our perspective on approaches for getting started, establishing the project leadership, seeking funding to support a project, recruiting and supporting faculty participants, developing strategies for running the program, and assessing the project's impact and making it visible on your campus.

First Steps

The first task in starting a campus program is to build interest among your faculty and administrators about the need for peer review and its potential impact on faculty development and student learning. Achieving this step involves demonstrating what the intellectual work of teaching looks like and how such work can be valuable for assessing student learning.

One approach is to invite a core group of your campus faculty to externally review some existing course portfolios, such as those on our project web site (www.courseportfolio.org). This process will help alleviate concerns that teaching cannot be documented because it is too ephemeral. Having them read a portfolio while using questions to guide their review begins to build an understanding of how course goals and student learning can be documented. It is also important that this core group meet to discuss what they have learned from the experience of writing a review: How did it help them to think about their own teaching? Did they see issues in the portfolios that connect to the challenges they face as teachers? Were they surprised by the quality and amount of student work expected of a particular course? In our experience, teachers who read and formally review a course portfolio have better insight into the process and understand better how a course portfolio might help them document and improve student learning. In the end, the key question for this group to address is whether this form of inquiry might be useful for developing, documenting, and assessing their own teaching and their students' learning.

Once faculty have seen the value of a course portfolio for documenting teaching, the next step is to encourage this core group of faculty to meet, interact, and write course portfolios for target courses of their own. It is especially valuable to have a small handful of "local" campus course portfolios that illustrate what peer review is and how it complements other teaching assessment approaches used on your campus. For instance, these examples could be compared with the common campus model of requiring a teaching portfolio for teaching award nominations or promotion. If developed electronically, your portfolios could be submitted to our project web site for posting or could be made available on your campus's computer network. Since the examples are local to your school, they will help demonstrate how this work has value for your faculty and will allow both colleagues and administrators to visualize the campus benefits that might occur if more faculty members became interested and active in this form of peer review.

As a third step, you could invite an outside speaker to introduce peer review of teaching to the campus through a seminar or workshop. This individual could also meet with you and with campus administrators to develop a campus implementation plan. There are trade-offs to inviting an outside speaker as a first step in the peer review process or as a last step. The benefit to starting a campus effort with an outside speaker is that he or she can generate enthusiasm for something new or can demonstrate how this work is part of cutting-edge national reform that might benefit your school. However, by coming later in the process, an outside speaker can often lend additional support to the work your core faculty group has already started by describing the peer review process at other schools and by connecting your campus's effort to the larger national teaching initiatives

The key task is to develop a core group of faculty who can share their work, help your administrators see the impact of the work, and start to engage your campus community.

Who Is Going to Run the Project?

At this point, it is important to decide who will run such a campus program and what type of funding is required to develop and support it.

You can take any one of a number of approaches to developing and organizing the project leadership of a campus program. Exhibit 7.1 lists common responsibilities and duties of project leaders. A key issue to decide is whether the program will be faculty-led or directed by someone from your school's professional or organizational development office (e.g., teaching and learning center, center for teaching excellence). Each approach has advantages and disadvantages. A faculty-led program often has a better connection between leaders and faculty participants since leaders, too, have to juggle your school's expectations for teaching, service, and research. The disadvantage is that many faculty leaders do not have experience in leading discussions on teaching and student learning, and so it may take some time for them to feel comfortable with facilitating and directing other faculty as they explore their teaching. In comparison, professional developers have the knowledge and resources such as secretarial staff and funds earmarked for teaching support to more easily assist faculty, but they often do not have the same level of in-class experience, or do not face the problems and questions (such as teaching a large class, teaching with technology, organizing student teams for a semester-long project) that faculty members deal with as they meet the challenges of teaching a course.

Exhibit 7.1 Typical Responsibilities and Duties of Peer Review Project Leaders

- Recruit faculty members for participation
- Plan meeting agendas
- Identify campus rooms and organize refreshments for events
- Order books and materials for faculty participants
- Develop and prepare project notebooks and handouts
- Identify articles and readings for meetings
- Lead or organize meeting discussions
- Coordinate the course portfolio development process
- Coordinate stipend payments to faculty participants
- Manage the project budget and expenses
- Send notices of project meetings
- Respond to questions from project participants
- Supervise the development and sharing of portfolios
- Maintain a project web site
- Communicate with administrators on the project status
- Assess project impact on teaching and student learning
- Seek internal and external funding sources for the project
- Disseminate project results to campus faculty and administrators

Both of these leadership approaches have been successfully used in our project consortium. Our project at the University of Nebraska–Lincoln and the project at the Kansas State University are both faculty-led. As such, teams of faculty organize and direct the project. To compensate faculty project leaders, we run the project over the academic year and then receive a stipend (a month of summer salary) as compensation for our time and effort. At the University of Michigan, Indiana University–Bloomington, and the University of Kansas, professional organizational developers from the university teaching and learning centers have coordinated and run the peer review projects. Texas A&M has created a unique model in which the lead coordinator is from the teaching and learning center, but she has recruited and partnered with two faculty members to co-coordinate the project with her. She has asked each of the faculty leaders' respective college deans to provide support (summer stipend money) for them to work with her as co-coordinators.

Where Is the Money?

While some level of financial commitment is necessary to support a peer review of teaching project, the amount varies depending on the size and scope of your program and the compensation you provide faculty participants. Exhibit 7.2 outlines components in a typical project budget.

Exhibit 7.2 Typical Project Budget Components for a Peer Review of Teaching Project

- Stipend to support project leaders
- Stipend to pay faculty participants
- Money to pay a support person (staff, graduate student, undergraduate student) to work with faculty in collecting materials and developing portfolios
- Money to pay a support person (staff, graduate student, undergraduate student) to help faculty scan examples of student work
- Funds to provide each participant a project notebook (with articles, readings, project materials)
- Money to support development of a web site for the posting of information materials and/or completed course portfolios
- Money to buy teaching-related books for faculty participants
- Money for providing refreshments at group meetings
- Travel money for project leaders to attend conferences and events
- Travel money for project participants to present their work at teaching and disciplinary meetings

Perhaps you are saying, "My school has no extra money. Is it really feasible to start a program like this?" The answer is yes. We encourage you to explore a number of funding sources. Exhibit 7.3 describes a few of those options. Be sure to work with your campus development office—these colleagues will know if your project would be of interest to particular individual, private, or corporate donors who have a special relationship with your institution.

Within our project consortium, each campus had success with different funding models. At the University of Nebraska–Lincoln and at Kansas State University, the project is funded directly by the provost or office of academic affairs. Since the University of Michigan, Indiana University–Bloomington, and University of Kansas administer their projects through their teaching and learning centers, the funding comes from their centers' budgets. Texas A&M's model is funded in part from their teaching and learning center and in part from the deans of the colleges whose faculty members participate in the program.

Exhibit 7.3 Possible Sources for Project Money

- Provost's office
- University foundation
- Local, regional, or national foundation
- Campus teaching and learning center
- Individual college deans
- Campus faculty teaching council

The largest item in our project budget is a stipend ($1,000) for each teacher who finishes a benchmark course portfolio. We have never felt that the actual dollar amount is central to motivating our project participants, and so $500 or even $250 may be equally meaningful to participants. Many of our faculty members use the money to pay for student support, travel, a new computer, or other research-related expenses. Others choose to take the money as salary. You might wonder, "Why do you pay faculty? Shouldn't evaluating and exploring one's own teaching and students' learning be part of the job of a teacher?" This is a good question, and the answer is not so simple. Developing a course portfolio and participating in project discussions of teaching are beyond the traditional level of reflection and assessment in which teachers typically engage. We have found that offering the stipend is a small thank-you for faculty participation and gives the project a higher priority in faculty members' busy lives. Although the sum is not large, it helps participants feel that the university administration backs their efforts to improve their teaching in a way similar to that by which research is rewarded through merit evaluations.

Beyond a stipend, there might be other ways to compensate faculty, such as travel funds, enhanced office or computer support, preference in picking a classroom, help from an undergraduate work-study student or a graduate research assistant, grading assistance, or lunch with the dean or provost. An obvious alternative is to reassign a portion of a faculty member's research or service time to their teaching and course development. This approach is parallel to the traditional academic model in which a faculty member's teaching time is reduced so that he or she can expand or refine research skills.

Is a peer review program feasible if you are unable to offer any compensation, monetary or otherwise, to faculty participants? It would work, but the campus impact probably would be limited. Chances are that your project participants would be the same faculty who attend and participate in all campus teaching efforts. But after their initial interest and participation, it would be hard to continue a sustained effort. Faculty who participate need tangible, concrete rewards and evidence that their participation is worthwhile. Building a campus culture around excellence in teaching requires these types of recognition.

Recruiting Project Participants

In creating a sustained campus effort for peer review of teaching, one of the key requirements is identifying campus faculty who want to participate. Exhibit 7.4 suggests several approaches for seeking interested faculty.

Exhibit 7.4 Approaches for Seeking Faculty Participants

- Personally inviting key department, college, and campus faculty

- Asking your school's faculty-led teaching council to solicit and recommend faculty
- Contacting department chairs and deans and asking them to nominate faculty
- Sending a solicitation through email (or campus mail) to all campus faculty
- Including an invitation in your campus faculty newspaper
- Having the student newspaper write a story about the program and recruitment

To recruit faculty members, you need to be able to share with them what outcomes they can anticipate from their participation. Exhibit 7.5 lists the goals we hope that faculty participants will achieve through our project. The most visible outcome is that each participant develops a benchmark course portfolio offering a careful investigation of student understanding and performance. When recruiting participants, we highlight how the course portfolio contrasts with the typical student evaluation of one's teaching. The portfolio is not meant to eliminate the student's voice but rather to narrow and focus the assessment of teaching in a form that explores the intellectual perspective in teaching a course. Just as importantly, faculty are engaged in cross-disciplinary conversations exploring questions regarding teaching and student learning and become motivated to increase their involvement in teaching initiatives across campus.

Exhibit 7.5 Outcomes From Faculty Participation

- Reflecting upon, developing, and writing a course portfolio about one of your courses
- Identifying common teaching and curricular issues with a department/ area peer
- Participating in interdisciplinary conversations about teaching and student learning
- Becoming skilled as a reader of a course portfolio

- Developing a common language/vocabulary about how to discuss the intellectual effort and scholarship of teaching
- Becoming part of a group of faculty who can create and advocate campus teaching policies

The big question that every faculty member asks is, "How much time will it take?" In our project, we estimate that participation takes about 50 hours of time over the nine months (August to May) of our project, an average of five to six hours a month. This estimate includes all of the time each person spends writing and participating in project meetings and discussions. Of course, the amount of time one puts into any of the peer review activities varies from person to person, although as we tell our students, the more time you can commit, the greater the learning experience. In a typical year, at least half of our 20 to 25 participants are pretenure faculty. Many of these faculty members comment that they have been told that their short-term focus should be on research and not teaching. While this attitude is common at many schools, we consider involvement in the project a powerful form of professional development for teaching, rather than as just added work. We have found that teachers who document their classroom goals, classroom methods, and the resulting student learning often have to spend far less time making changes in subsequent course offerings. As a result, the up-front expenditure of time typically has a large payoff in their professional work as teachers and thus gives them more time for doing research.

You can focus recruitment around individual faculty, disciplinary pairs of faculty, or larger department teams. Exhibit 7.6 highlights the advantages and disadvantages of each approach. Participation in our project is completely voluntary and is open to all individuals actively teaching students. Previous participants have included administrators, department chairs, tenured faculty, tenure-track faculty, lecturers, adjunct faculty members, and graduate teaching assistants. Originally, our project focused on recruiting large department teams in the hopes of having a significant impact on the teaching culture of an entire department. While we had much success, after a couple of years we realized that we were excluding a significant number of campus faculty who would not be able to assemble a large department team. As a consequence, our current approach is to seek disciplinary pairs for participation. This also allows us to recruit participants from departments where a significant proportion of faculty have already gone through peer review. We also accept larger department teams, but we subdivide these teams into pairs. When individual faculty members sign up for the project with no partner, we team them with another "single" participant from a related disciplinary area.

Exhibit 7.6 Type's of Faculty Participants

Type of Faculty	Advantage	Disadvantage
Individual faculty member	Easier to identify and secure for participation	Without a defined disciplinary partner, a faculty member can feel isolated during group conversations and in sharing work with others
Disciplinary pairs	Since the partners can read and discuss disciplinary aspects of their courses, they are better able to explore connections between courses	It can be difficult to find a partner in a department that is small or that doesn't recognize or value efforts to improve teaching. Also, a junior faculty member might be uncomfortable in asking a senior faculty person to be his or her partner.
Larger department teams	Conversations can expand beyond individual courses to linkages across department courses and the overall curriculum	Recruiting a large team can be challenging. Some programs are small and trying to recruit a larger team can lead faculty to join from peer pressure rather than a desire to explore their teaching.

Since our project operates from August to May, we start to recruit faculty in the late spring and throughout the summer. Our goal is to identify all participants before the start of the fall academic semester. This approach excludes new faculty who join the school over the summer months and do not hear about the project. While this is a consideration, we have observed that new campus faculty have many other issues facing them during their first year on campus, and so their efforts are often better focused elsewhere. In fact, many of the junior faculty who have participated in our project have commented that their first year of teaching helped them to articulate and define the classroom and student learning issues and challenges that they were uncomfortable with and that they chose to explore during their subsequent participation in the project.

Strategies for Running a Project

A key component of running a project is developing and disseminating the project calendar. Such a calendar informs possible participants of the time investment required by outlining all the meeting dates and project requirements. While there are other approaches for running a project—making the project only a semester long, or focusing it all in a one-week summer retreat—we have chosen to spread out our project agenda over the entire academic year, so that faculty have the time to reflect and write about their teaching in a systematic way. In addition, we have found that allowing time to lapse between discussions and writing activities helps faculty to better refine ideas and thoughts about their teaching. Exhibit 7.7 provides an overview of our yearlong calendar.

Exhibit 7.7 Typical Project Calendar for the Academic Year

Month	Time	Description
August	3-hour meeting the week prior to classes starting	Entire group meets for the project orientation; introduce participants to the project and get them talking and generating concerns/ideas about their teaching

Month	Time	Description
September	4-hour retreat on a Saturday	Entire group meets to discuss readings from provided books and to spend focused time writing interaction 1
October	1 hour during the week	Team partners meet to discuss Benchmark Memo 1
October	1 hour during the week	Project leaders meet individually with each team to discuss Benchmark Memos 1 and 2
November	1.5-hour meeting during the week	Entire group meets to discuss readings and share issues and insights
January	1.5-hour meeting during the week	Entire group meets to discuss readings and to be introduced to the concept of collecting data from their courses
January	1 hour during the week	Team partners meet to discuss Benchmark Memo 2
March	1 hour during the week	Project leaders meet individually with each team to discuss Benchmark Memo 3
April	4-hour retreat on a Saturday	Entire group meets to discuss readings from provided books and to spend focused time writing interaction 3
May	2-day workshop (4 hours each day) on the Monday and Tuesday after final exams	Entire group meets to discuss readings from provided books and to spend focused time linking materials into course portfolios
June	Portfolio due	Completed portfolios are due and posted on project web site

As the calendar shows, we have a project orientation meeting the week before classes begin in the fall. Each of the faculty participants selects one of their upcoming spring courses as a target course. During the fall semester, each participant writes Benchmark Memos 1 and 2 for this course. We have found that writing these memos in the fall semester allows a faculty member to make changes to course design and assessment strategies prior to collecting data on student learning. During the fall semester, participants also meet with their department peer(s) and the larger project group to discuss their writing, talk about assigned readings, and debate questions regarding teaching and student learning. During the spring semester, each participant teaches their target course and collects examples of student learning. Participants also continue to meet with their peers and with the larger group to discuss issues related to student learning in the target courses, such as "What is student learning in my course? Am I achieving it? How do I document it?" Toward the end of the spring semester, each participant writes Benchmark Memo 3. At the conclusion of the semester, participants attend a focused workshop during which they integrate their materials to create a benchmark course portfolio and explore the cross-disciplinary aspects of learning how others teach.

We have several key activities to support faculty as they write their memos and create their course portfolios. We host three faculty retreats over the course of the academic year. The first is held in September and focuses on assisting faculty as they write Benchmark Memo 1 (goals for their course). The second is in April and supports faculty as they write Benchmark Memo 3 (showcasing student learning). The final workshop, held in May, helps faculty as they link their three memos together into a course portfolio. The first two retreats are held on Saturdays, while the final retreat is a part of the project workshop after the spring semester is over. While a Saturday meeting might be unusual for academics, we have had much success with these retreats. In our experience, faculty need focused time to think about their course and to write these memos. Consequently we schedule the retreats in rooms with computer access so that faculty can write their memos in a community of other teachers without the typical daily distractions.

Each May, we hire a student to individually meet and work with faculty to collect their course portfolio materials. Having a single contact person who is responsible for collecting, assembling, preparing the materials, and scanning student work has been very successful. It allows a faculty member to focus on the big ideas in regard to the course while the student worker can handle the secretarial aspects of organizing the portfolio.

Once a faculty member has completed the project, we not only provide the faculty stipend, but each participant receives a formal letter acknowledging and thanking them for their work. Our school's senior vice chancellor for academic affairs (i.e., the provost) also sends each participant a letter recognizing their accomplishment. This letter gives faculty members concrete and explicit recognition of their project accomplishments that they can easily share with a department chair and/or include in annual review materials or promotion and tenure documentation. While we do not do so, one could also provide each participant with a framed certificate signifying his or her accomplishment.

Seeking External Reviews of Portfolios

If you are seeking a single review for your own course portfolio or for that of a colleague, the process is typically straightforward. Reviewers can be identified and the review facilitated through contacts and personal requests. Project administrators may find it more difficult if they need to seek dozens of reviews each year. In these cases, they must address several important logistical questions, including the following:

- Should a reviewer's identity be kept confidential from a portfolio author?

- Who gets to see a review? A formative review will obviously be read by the portfolio author. Will this also be true for a summative review?

- Should someone (such as the program director) decide if a portfolio is "worthy" of external review? This would be analogous to the procedure in which an editor or associate editor of a scholarly publication assesses a submission before sending the article to reviewers. What do you do with a portfolio that fails this first step?

- Should reviewers be compensated for their time (e.g., money, gift certificates, letters of recognition, reciprocal reviews of their portfolios)? While reviewing a text manuscript is typically compensated, writing a review of a scholarly publication or grant application often has no direct compensation. The inferred payoff is that by reviewing you will submit a future publication or grant application to the organization.

The answer to the above questions will be specific to your individual program, school, and role of the external review. In our project, we keep reviewers' identities anonymous. Reviews are formative, thus they are seen by the portfolio author. We do not currently apply any editorial standard to judge the quality of a portfolio before sending it for review. Finally, we send each external reviewer a thank-you letter, but do not provide any financial compensation.

Measuring and Disseminating the Project's Impact

Regardless of how you organize the day-to-day administration of your program, its success will depend on how well faculty and administrators value its impact on faculty development and student learning. Just as we assess student learning in our classrooms, it is important to plan and assess the impact of your project by collecting ongoing qualitative and quantitative data from faculty participants. Exhibit 7.8 outlines qualitative questions we have asked former participants after they have completed the project. Another important part of qualitative assessment is to assemble a list of faculty project work that has been published or presented at disciplinary or teaching conferences. These details will help document and highlight the regional and national impact of your project.

Exhibit 7.8 Assessment Questions

1) In which contexts have you used the teaching insights you gained from your participation in the Peer Review of Teaching Project?

2) In which contexts have you used the course portfolio you created during your participation in the Peer Review of Teaching Project?

3) If you have used your course portfolio, how was it received by others? For example, did readers think it was strong evidence of the intellectual work of teaching?

4) How has your teaching changed as a result of your participation in the Peer Review of Teaching Project? What has been the impact on student learning in your courses?

5) As an outgrowth of your involvement with peer review, have you participated in any other department, college, or campus initiatives designed to support/improve teaching and learning? Briefly summarize.

6) Indicate your agreement (strongly agree, agree, indifferent, disagree, strongly disagree, not applicable) to the following statements: My participation in the Peer Review of Teaching Project has been useful in ...

    - Helping me to improve my teaching in my target course (the one I focused my project participation on)

    - Helping me to improve my teaching in other courses I teach

    - Helping me to develop better methods for documenting and analyzing my teaching and the resulting student learning

    - Helping me to identify, articulate, and revise course goals and learning objectives

    - Helping me to identify an issue in my teaching and to develop a plan for investigating it

    - Fostering self-reflection and awareness about my own teaching practices

    - Building a vocabulary for discussing and evaluating teaching as intellectual work

    - Developing a sense of what constitutes an effective course portfolio

    - Providing structures and strategies for creating a course portfolio

    - Developing a sense of how to read and assess others' teaching materials

    - Generating strategies for integrating the documentation of teaching into my classroom practices

    - Helping me/my department to identify and revise curricular goals/practices across departmental courses

    - Providing me opportunities to learn about teaching issues in other academic areas/departments

    - Becoming part of a group of faculty who can create and advocate campus teaching policies

    - Developing leadership skills in supporting and improving teaching at the campus level

Two key quantitative metrics are the number of faculty participants and the number of course portfolios developed in the project. While it might seem that this should be one and the same, this is not necessarily the case. Faculty members have busy lives, and sometimes they need additional motivation to encourage them to finish their course portfolio, even though they derive other benefits from participating in the project. To help alleviate this problem, we have learned several lessons. First, set a deadline for faculty to complete their portfolio. Faculty members are not unlike students, and deadlines are great motivators. Second, never authorize recognition (faculty stipend, congratulatory letter, travel money, and the like) until a portfolio is complete and turned in.

Once data is collected, it is important to share the results with administrators and the overall campus community. Exhibit 7.9 provides some strategies for achieving this.

Exhibit 7.9 Strategies for Publicizing the Project and Its Impact

- Hold a presentation on campus
- Recruit faculty participants to present their work at a faculty meeting
- Hold a campus teaching conference or workshop
- Invite campus administrators to a project meeting and let them hear stories and comments about how the project has impacted faculty teaching
- Publish and distribute a newsletter highlighting the project and sharing faculty quotes on the impact of the project
- Distribute announcements to faculty listservs and newsletters with links to the project web site

Final Thoughts on Starting a Peer Review Project

Any project that you develop will be unique to your school and its faculty. This chapter has highlighted some of the key issues and decisions involved in starting and running a campus program. Before you say "no thank you," we can tell you that in retrospect, few of us thought that we would be running a faculty development program. Yet all of us have found satisfaction in helping establish a campus program that has had an impact on hundreds of faculty participants, on our school, and most importantly, on ourselves. It has been a rewarding experience for professional and personal growth that none of us would trade. Should you take the lead on your campus, we wish you the best of luck and encourage you to contact us or one of our partner campus project leaders for support, advice, and feedback. The contact details for all of the project leaders are available on our project web site (www.courseportfolio.org).

What's Next

This chapter has focused on highlighting issues involved in starting a campus peer review of teaching project. The next chapter will explore institutional issues and emerging national issues and trends related to peer review and its connection to the scholarship of teaching and learning.

8 ADDRESSING LARGER ISSUES IN PEER REVIEW

Thus far, we have focused on practical questions such as how to write and review course portfolios and how to promote collaboration around teaching with faculty peers. But you might also be thinking about larger questions, such as the place of peer review in a professional academic career or in an institution. You might be wondering about institutional issues, such as the use of electronic portfolios, addressing cooperation with students for consideration of their work, the use of peer review in personnel matters, or the potential use of peer review in accreditation. Or you might be thinking beyond your institution to issues of a national scope, such as whether course portfolios are considered scholarship, the place of cross-institutional repositories of teaching and learning, issues of intellectual property, and partnerships with institutional review boards.

This chapter focuses on these topics that are especially important to faculty members who wish to initiate peer collaboration, to faculty leaders who want to start a program of peer review, and to administrative leaders who would like to integrate substantive peer review in their institution's procedures. For those who are committed to developing and sustaining peer collaboration on and review of teaching in an institution, this chapter speaks to promoting an institutional culture, or climate, of teaching excellence and to participating in conversations about teaching reforms and professional development across postsecondary education. We offer a set of recommendations for the institutional-level support of the peer review of teaching, and we discuss some key issues for the peer review of teaching as it becomes a national movement. We close with an invitation to campus leaders.

Impact of Peer Review on Students' Learning

Peer review of teaching does not entail a heavy time burden beyond the work a faculty member already engages in. Faculty members will create syllabi, plan and spend time with students in classes and studios, and create and evaluate assignments, whether or not this work is shared with colleagues. Capturing this work and reflecting on it requires some time, but it is a small proportion of the total time that one devotes to teaching. Still, it is reasonable to ask whether this modest marginal cost entailed in peer review has any benefits for students' learning. Faculty members, students, and the institution have an interest in this result, and it could be argued that no one should spend additional time on an extra teaching activity unless learning is enhanced.

In the first several years of our project we had support from the U.S. Department of Education (Fund for the Improvement of Postsecondary Education) to monitor carefully the impact of participation in the peer review program. Graduate students collected a rich portfolio of documentation of the courses taught by the faculty participants, including syllabi, assignments, and student work. Based on a review of educational research on teaching effectiveness, we categorized the teaching methods used in the classes as more or less likely to generate learning. We used a consensus taxonomy of levels of understanding to describe both what the professors were asking of students and what the students were doing. As reported in Bernstein, Jonson, and Smith (2000), we were able to compare the behavior of teachers and learners before and after their participation in the peer review process.

For those faculty members who changed their teaching practices, there was a clear improvement in the amount of student learning and in the depth of their learning. Students were challenged to do more demanding intellectual work, and a larger percentage achieved at advanced levels (Bernstein et al., 2000). Including the peer review process described in this volume did generate enhanced learning, and we believe that this result justifies the small extra time required. These data demonstrated that an institution could use routine course portfolio procedures to document its programmatic success without creating a new layer of educational measurement or bureaucracy. If faculty members simply keep copies of the work that students already do, complete with the evaluation of its intellectual merit that they already do, the resulting archive provides the opportunity to evaluate a claim of effective learning.

There are many contexts in which institutions are called upon to demonstrate that their fundamental mission is being accomplished. No matter what else happens at a university, students should be acquiring intellectual knowledge and skills. Wergin (2005a, 2005b) describes the challenge that higher education faces in convincing the public to continually increase support for higher education. Only by opening up the process of learning and showing the evidence of student success can these questions be properly addressed. The institution can present itself very well to its constituents by making the learning of its students visible to all interested parties. Leaders can support the widespread use of course portfolios that include samples of student work, and they can invite faculty peers and general community members to consider this evidence of institutional success.

The challenge from the early peer review program, however, was that less than half of the faculty participants made any detectable changes in how they taught as a result of their participation. Only when peer review resulted in changed teaching methods was there a resulting enhancement in the learning success of the community. For institutions, the message seems clear: It is not enough to support faculty members in conversations about how teaching might be done differently. Institutions need to arrange meaningful consequences for those faculty members who go beyond the conversation and actually enact teaching practices informed by educational research. Peer review of intellectual practices in teaching can truly enhance learning for students, but this change will happen only when institutions notice and honor those faculty members who use the process to make changes in their teaching. Simply having faculty members participate in good conversations about teaching does not magically transform learning by students.

Institutional Issues in Peer Review

Campus leaders have many reasons for wanting their institution's teaching and learning to be visible to the community. For example, any consistent or systematic plan for demonstrating the intellectual value of a degree from an institution must begin with an examination of how students perform in their courses. Similarly, any plan to improve the level of student learning over time must make visible the trajectory of levels of learning students achieve in the institution's courses.

In the same way that any research enterprise benefits from open discussion of the emerging results of ongoing inquiry, an institution needs to have its learning products visible to the whole community for consideration. Shulman's (1999) essay on the scholarship of teaching and learning identifies the accessibility of artifacts of teaching and learning as the defining characteristic of scholarly work. The conversation and discussion around the understanding demonstrated by learners should drive the search for methods to further enhance learning. To help assure that learning and teaching are visible on its campus, an institution can take a number of steps, from supporting a forum for faculty conversation to using course portfolios in review of academic units.

Support a Forum for Faculty Conversations

The core of the peer review process is frequent interaction among faculty colleagues about their teaching and their students' learning. Thus, at a most basic level, an institution needs to support communication by supporting opportunities for faculty conversations. These conversations are hard to fit into the full and busy lives of contemporary faculty members, as they have more opportunities for productive activities than they have time to complete them. Providing small resources for faculty members who do participate is an important way that an institution can capture faculty attention to teaching. Leaders can also publicly honor those who take time away from other academic pursuits to work on the effectiveness of their teaching.

Faculty members' communication about teaching can begin with an exchange of written materials and mutual reaction through written reply, then develop into face-to-face conversations. In our project, we have found that faculty members' increasing skill and comfort with technology shaped how we facilitated communication focused on teaching. Although we initially asked faculty members to exchange memos on paper using conventional mail, our participants quickly began using email for their interactions instead. By simply copying project leaders on each email, they helped us create an archive of the written work done in response to the three memos (prompts for interaction). After a few semesters, we realized that the threaded discussion feature of any course management tool provided a perfect environment for managing and conserving the interactions around peer review. We learned that a complete round of initial memos and reply memos could be nicely punctuated with a face-to-face meeting. Further, because these live conversations, often in groups related to an academic unit or program, were based upon shared experience and knowledge from the written memos, there was no need for a lengthy presentation time. The group meetings were thus lively and informed, with the technologically supported exchange providing a great start to the conversation.

Help Make Course Portfolios Visible

The essence of our community building is that faculty members' writing about their teaching becomes a visible intellectual product that is discussed like any other. Thus a key component for institutional support is making faculty members' portfolios visible. At our institution, we decided that electronic distribution would foster the greatest accessibility for these intellectual products. We could only make such a decision because the university provided a technological infrastructure and access to technical staff to support this work.

When we recognized that faculty participants were composing their portfolios electronically, it made no sense to print them out for sharing. Paper portfolios are difficult to transport and expensive to deliver to colleagues on other campuses. Instead, we began to circulate the portfolios in electronic format, allowing for wider, quicker, and cheaper distribution, and increased accessibility in accord with Shulman's (1999) call for the work to be learned from, critically reviewed, and built upon. About the same time, we observed the growing use of electronic portfolios for both student and faculty intellectual work (especially those in the Visible Knowledge Project at Georgetown University's Center for New Designs in Learning and Scholarship), and we decided to develop a format for electronic course portfolios.

Once the work was placed on a web site, two advantages appeared immediately. First, it was possible to give other faculty broad and easy access to the work; the distribution was seamless, inexpensive, and fast. Second, we were able to take full advantage of the hypertext nature of these documents, and readers were able to move around within the materials on their own. Rather than recreating only the traditional linear text common to academic writing, our participants had the option of inviting readers to leave the primary narrative and go into more depth on a particular aspect of the course. For example, a reader who teaches a similar course could easily go to the portfolio author's archive and see samples of assignment prompts and student work before continuing with the narrative account. This electronic format also gave some faculty members more freedom to display their student work in a complex and rich way that conventional paper presentations did not readily support. In the long run, the use of photographs, sound and video recordings, downloadable student presentations, or links to web-based resources and student work greatly enhances portfolio authors' abilities to fully and richly represent the accomplishments and learning of their students.

A final advantage of the electronic course portfolio is found in its essential flexibility. The form is readily updated and expandable, allowing faculty members to add student work and reflection from subsequent semesters. This format captures the metaphor of teaching as inquiry; the course portfolio is not a static document but a living repository of the ongoing work of a teacher. This format invites people to represent a trajectory of their success in promoting student learning, and as such it is the ideal vehicle for representing the kind of reflective practice in teaching that many consider a desirable standard for higher education.

We have learned a number of practical lessons in the process of designing an electronic portfolio format. We originally put course portfolios in HTML format, and hyperlinks allowed readers to access the multiple pages of the portfolio and view the student examples. Once prepared, the resulting portfolio could be sent electronically to another person and was easily accessible over the Internet. But we found that HTML was not ideal for formatting advanced text such as mathematic equations, and it did not yield the highest quality visual images. We also learned that many portfolio readers preferred to read from a printed text rather than from a computer screen, and so they wanted the portfolio to be easy to print out. After considering many options, we converted all portfolios into Adobe Portable Document Format (PDF) files for distribution. This format has several advantages.

- *Simplified portfolio distribution:* Authors can share their portfolios by disk, by sending them electronically, or by posting them on a web site.

- *Ease of sharing portfolios:* Anyone can open Adobe PDF documents on any computer system—regardless of the software platform, the original application, or the availability of specific fonts—using the free Adobe Reader software.

- *Preserving the look and integrity of the original portfolio:* Adobe PDF files look exactly like the original pages as the authors created them.

- *Searching:* Adobe PDF files allow searches for words or phrases appearing in the portfolio.

- *Bookmarking:* Authors can easily add bookmarks within an Adobe PDF file to mimic the hyperlink capability of web pages so that a reader can quickly jump to different parts of the portfolio.

- *Zooming:* A reader can easily increase or decrease the magnification view so as to be able to better see portfolio materials.

Whatever approach a campus takes for the distribution of course portfolios, the key is to make them broadly accessible for use and review by others. Integration of our peer review process with the campus's instructional technology resources made it possible to create and sustain a community to support teaching. Even when we had outside consultants work on our site design, there was close and supportive collaboration with campus instructional technology staff.

Support Sensitive Treatment of Student Work

Student performance that demonstrates their understanding forms the centerpiece of our model of a course portfolio. Recent discussions about student work, intellectual property, and the ethics of research with human participants have begun to address how to make visible students' performance in a respectful, proper, and ethical manner. An all-purpose reference for these practices is *Ethics of Inquiry: Issues in the Scholarship of Teaching and Learning* (Hutchings, 2002).

On a local level, the institutional leadership should help develop a set of general guidelines for the creation of learning archives. It would be inefficient for every faculty member to negotiate individually with ethics committees about the nuts and bolts of obtaining permission and procedures for managing privacy. Proactive institutional support and policies make it much easier for all concerned and also saves a lot of human time by both teachers and review committee members.

As a general rule, we recommend that faculty members ask students' permission to use their work as part of an archive for a course. Faculty members can keep, without students' permission, a copy of student work to use for their own development as a teacher, including the sharing of anonymous work with colleagues in a private conversation. When that work may become part of a presentation or publication, however, or if that work is represented in any public setting such as a web site, then formal written consent is necessary.

As the consent form reproduced in Chapter 2 illustrates, we recommend that students have the option to retain their names on their work, providing them with the opportunity to take full credit for their creative or intellectual product. Projects such as essays, poems, artwork, advertising materials, and product designs are all examples of work that students may wish to have recognized as their own. It is especially good to gather student permission in such a way that the teacher does not know until after the course is completed which students have given permission to make their work public. This preserves the voluntary nature of the students' choice in granting permission for public use.

Some faculty members find it daunting to ask for students' consent in this way, especially given the uncertainty that the archive will be usable in public venues. A professor in industrial engineering expressed this concern:

> I was worried that if I told my students I was writing a course portfolio, they would immediately question my abilities as their teacher. I also was concerned that none of my students would give me permission. To my surprise, I got all the forms back and all of them gave permission. In fact, my students were incredibly engaged and excited to learn that I was interested in improving

the course by tracking and assessing their learning. As a result, throughout the semester, they often wanted me to give them an update on what I had learned so far.

This faculty member's initial hesitation and her students' reactions are quite common. Many teachers find that describing their participation in peer review spurs their students to become more vocal about their perspectives and concerns. Even though all the students in this teacher's class agreed to participate, it is important to communicate to students that participation is entirely voluntary and that they can choose not to participate without penalty. Since the faculty member will not receive information about individual permission until after the course is completed, there is no opportunity for or appearance of forced cooperation.

A second concern involves the campus committee for the review of research with human participants (referred to in some places as human subjects). While the original law creating these oversight committees, formally known as Institutional Review Boards (IRBs), stated that educational research was to be exempt from such review, recent federal government practice has expanded the range of that oversight to require that IRBs review any work that may ultimately be treated as research. Any faculty member who plans to give a conference presentation or other public rendering of teaching work should follow the guidelines of the local IRB for reporting the activity and obtaining permission from the institution.

We can make no uniform recommendation concerning whether to seek IRB approval, since the specific policies differ from school to school. At a minimum, though, students must have given informed consent to the teacher to collect and include their work in a public course portfolio. It has been the practice at the University of Nebraska–Lincoln that merely placing student work into a course portfolio requires permission from the student but not approval by the IRB. Students' work being included in a course portfolio does not magically transform teaching into research, but many institutions consider anything published or presented at a conference to be research, by definition. All faculty members should be familiar with the policies of the local IRB and follow them. When there is a procedure for obtaining permission from the students already in place, there should be no problem in obtaining approval from any IRB under their "exempt" category. Campus leadership on this matter can create general guidelines that will allow sharing of evidence of learning without extensive individual negotiation of terms.

Integrate Peer Review of Teaching Into Campus Personnel Decisions

A crucial measure of the success of peer review of teaching will be its seamless integration into the personnel evaluation systems of most universities. Teaching in higher education is often evaluated mostly based on the satisfaction surveys completed by students, with an overlay of peer observation of faculty performance during class time. Many universities have recently added language to their teaching materials that encourages the scholarship of teaching and learning, but too often this simply means granting some credit toward scholarly productivity for articles, chapters, and books written about teaching. As discussed later in this chapter, the transformation of teaching into a research enterprise may not be desirable, and it is not the primary focus of the project we have developed.

Instead, we suggest that reflective course portfolios representing multiple semesters of teaching be included as elements in the larger teaching portfolio or dossier that goes forward for evaluation of each faculty member's performance. These course portfolios can be given an external, arm's-length review by established teachers in the same field. The resulting commentary can be parallel to the ubiquitous letters from outside scholars that evaluate the quality and productivity of research done by faculty members up for tenure or promotion. Some may object to this suggestion, pointing to the time and effort required to generate and refine a course portfolio, as well as expressing concern about the availability of appropriate reviewers for so many portfolios.

It may take a significant amount of time to transform the usual products of teaching into a course portfolio, but that amount of time appears at least commensurate with the amount of time a faculty member might devote to writing and publishing a report of his or her research. Most researchers would be delighted if they could go from finishing the collection of evidence to completed public representation of a research project in 15 to 20 hours, the time our participants report that they usually need to write a course portfolio. The time required to review a portfolio and write an evaluative memo is also variable, but in the experience of our reviewers, it takes roughly the same amount of time as reviewing a typical journal article submitted for publication. If one truly values the peer perspective on the quality of all intellectual work, there is no compelling reason not to offer the same reading time to evaluating teaching that is routinely given to evaluating research done by colleagues all over the globe.

The availability of reviewers is not a trivial problem, as many people recognize that faculty members everywhere are spending more time than ever evaluating each other's work, whether for funding projects, awards, annual review or accountability, or major career steps such as tenure or promotion. We do not wish to dismiss this realistic concern. What is sometimes not appreciated, however, is that not everyone in the academic profession is called upon to review research work, often because those people are spending the majority of their work time on the many activities that teaching entails. A large population of professionals throughout the academic community has focused on teaching and could make time for reviewing other faculty members' teaching. It could even be argued that those faculty members who focus on the teaching portion of their profession would be preferable to have as external reviewers. The additional reviewing need not come from the same pool of readers that is already reviewing other forms of intellectual work.

The final key for efficiency at the institutional level is an explicit alignment of the processes of departmental annual review, campus review for awards, and institutional review for promotion or tenure. If departments based annual review of teaching on course portfolios and occasional reactions of outside readers, they would have an accumulating file of portfolios and substantive evaluations for each faculty member. Teaching award committees could have easy access to the body of portfolios to complement the many testimonial letters praising the dedication, accessibility, and humanity of each nominee. If an institution maintained the habit of periodically obtaining outside evaluations of the work in each course portfolio, then this accessible file would already be in place to be part of the teaching award committee's deliberations. Finally, if departments and larger units such as colleges or schools kept these electronic course portfolios as part of the permanent record of each faculty member, the cumulative body of work could be examined again at times of major personnel decisions. An enormous amount of time and work would be saved by using the same forms and reviews for all three processes of evaluating teaching. Since the content of a course portfolio is so rich, an institution can use it for several forms of evaluation of teaching simultaneously. Measured against its potential for use, the portfolio requires only a small investment of time. Material can be prepared once and used for multiple purposes over a period of years.

Of course, a possible tension can arise when a single activity or product is used both for evaluating and improving teaching. Some faculty members believe that meaningful growth in teaching development best occurs when teachers are in a safe community in which weaknesses and issues to be improved can be freely mentioned and addressed. Peer review used in a personnel process has an explicit frame of judgment about quality, and some people feel that those conditions limit real growth. At the same time, most schools operate under the premise that research gets better when it is open for critical review and assessment by colleagues. Rather than framing peer review as a form of surveillance, then, we frame it as a process that offers multiple opportunities for engagement and inquiry into one's teaching within a community of peers, both locally and nationally, depending upon one's purposes and needs as a teacher.

Careful attention to process can help faculty develop work done for improvement of teaching into a product that can be useful in evaluation (Bernstein, 1996). In our version of peer review, faculty members write about their teaching and privately exchange memos and course portfolios with colleagues. The readers' comments go only to the author of the course, not to a designated senior colleague or chair or dean. The teacher can take advantage of this private exchange to make changes in his or her teaching and in the formal representation of the teaching via the course portfolio, improving both over time. Only on occasions for formal evaluation of teaching does the faculty member bring forward a mature, refined course portfolio to represent her or his teaching. A benchmark portfolio could reflect the instructor's current level of success in promoting student understanding, and an inquiry portfolio could make visible a trajectory of improvement in understanding that shows his or her own thoughtful learning.

Consider the similar relationship between growth and evaluation in the area of research. Scholars participate in brown-bag conversations about their work, present preliminary results and analyses at colloquia and conferences, and then revise their manuscripts based on feedback and reviews until they are ready for publication. When asked to show the quality of their research, they bring forward only the finished product, and the growth and development from prior interaction with colleagues is not visible to evaluators. We offer the course portfolio as a parallel summary product of the intellectual work in teaching. The faculty member reflects and acts on feedback in an informal, private context and brings forward the finished product when a public representation of his or her work is needed for evaluation.

Use Portfolios in Analyzing Academic Units

Institutions typically conduct periodic examination of the activities of their academic units such as departments or programs. Often these academic program reviews (APRs) involve an enormous amount of time as unit members gather evidence and organize it for local and outside reviewers. Faculty members and unit leaders spend considerable time reflecting on the evidence and learning from it, and that time is seen as well spent, but the time and energy devoted to gathering and organizing data is rarely perceived to be inherently valuable. A systematic presentation of the materials found in course portfolios would provide a ready source of information about student learning in the unit, which is the primary product of the teaching mission. If a unit routinely kept course portfolios from strategically identified courses, the analysis of the state of learning in the unit would be much simpler. If the unit engaged in systematic reflection on those materials between APRs, the reporting for the teaching part of the exercise would be quite simple. The faculty and leaders of the unit would already have identified where in the program student learning was strongest and where student learning might be increased through enhanced efforts.

On many occasions during the Peer Review of Teaching Project at the University of Nebraska–Lincoln, teams of faculty members from a single unit have exchanged course portfolios for the purpose of conducting an analysis of learning at a unit level, rather than at the level of the individual teacher or course. These examples provided a number of insights that would not have been reached without having the course portfolios as the basic evidence for consideration. Each of these units contributed an example of work that enhanced student performance in lower-division classes and that increased faculty engagement in the success of general education at the university. While the particular accomplishments varied across units, the basic program of public consideration of student performance in course portfolios remained a constant centerpiece of this academic process. The following examples show the power of these public conversations about portfolios.

Visual Literacy

Several departments that shared an interest in foundational skill in visual arts had combined efforts to offer a common introductory course; students in photography, art, architecture, and textile design all learned basics of color and form through a team-taught course in visual literacy. However, the course was foundering, and faculty members in several units were losing confidence in the coherence and value of the requirement. The four visual literacy faculty members used their participation in the peer review project as an opportunity to consider the hard questions of exactly what they were trying to accomplish in the course and exactly how they would know if they succeeded.

The result of their inquiry was a clear common syllabus and an agreed-upon grading rubric for the course assignments. Student reaction was overwhelmingly positive as the course goals became clear to them, and other faculty in the departments were more satisfied with the course products. Not only was the course preserved and enhanced, but several of the team members have presented their work at professional meetings as a model of collaboration on student learning among artists.

Political Science

A team including the department chair documented student learning in some of the core courses in the major, including lower-division courses that met the university's general educational goals. The group conversations were quite revealing as faculty learned about one another's student performance for the first time. Some faculty members learned that their students' work was exceptionally good, while others learned that they needed to raise their expectations. The view of teaching and learning across the department was so clear that the chair made collaborative consideration of student learning standard practice and required all untenured faculty members to go through the process at least once before tenure.

English

The English department team included faculty members on different sides of a department split about the goals of composition classes. They were not initially in agreement about what to look for in writing, perhaps one of the most important of all general educational skills. Their formal written interactions about one another's goals and graded student work were the most prolific and substantive of any department, and like the artists, they tackled the difficult intellectual work of articulating their criteria for grading writing. The products of those conversations are among the most impressive models of course portfolios that came from the project, and they reached a deeper understanding of the varying types of intellectual goals in this course. Their articulation of the reasons for varying grades in writing assignments stands as a model for the university's faculty, and those sections of their now-public syllabi are often referred to by faculty from many other departments. Perhaps most challenging, they agreed upon a proposal for a new required course in the English major, and in the succeeding year, their collective support helped gain department acceptance of the newly recommended curriculum change.

Mathematics

The mathematics department wanted to create some consensus among the many faculty members who were teaching the entry-level calculus courses that served general education for most University of Nebraska–Lincoln students. With as many as eight different teachers each year, the department saw inconsistency in the work required of students and in the grading standards, despite having a commonly agreed-upon set of midsemester examinations. When these faculty members viewed shared examples of graded exams from other sections, they had their first frank conversations about what a passing grade in calculus really means. The net result was a general raising of the level of performance accepted as passing, with a clearer community understanding of the standards used in these prerequisite courses. The department chair was especially pleased that the process yielded a consensus course portfolio for each of two classes, so that the content of these general education service courses would not vary so widely, even as the lead instructor changed from semester to semester.

Psychology

The psychology team worked on two perennial issues in curriculum planning: improving the quality of writing in a large introductory class and coordinating the accomplishment of curricular goals in classes that are linked in content. The faculty members' focused interactions on student performance led to changes in both the teaching method and the success of this widely subscribed general education course.

After faculty members exchanged their memos for the first interaction (focused on content goals), they redistributed topics between a lower-division course in learning and its upper-division cousin, eliminating redundancy and more rationally ordering topics. Moreover, when the two instructors of those courses checked to see if students in the second course still remembered the work they had done in the first course, the results were disappointing. The ensuing departmental conversation resulted in changes in the first course (including swapping instructors), with the result that student retention of learning from the first course to the second was improved. When the professor teaching the introductory course learned from her participation in the department conversations about methods of student-to-student sharing of term paper drafts, she added this relatively simple procedure to the introductory course. Performance on the instructor-graded term paper increased a full grade level on average for this 300-student lecture course.

As these examples suggest, faculty conversations and the exchange of materials around student learning serve more than one function. While they are initially generated to provide helpful feedback for teachers, the later versions of portfolios can serve as meaningful evidence of excellence in teaching and learning. It is a good idea for institutions to encourage efficient use of documentation already generated, as long as faculty members retain the ultimate choice about how their course portfolios are used. The tension between developing teaching and evaluating teaching can be managed (Bernstein, 1996), and institutional leaders should welcome the presentation of such evidence without mandating that it be reported.

Consider and Address Faculty Members' Questions About the Peer Review of Teaching

Most postsecondary teachers are not inclined toward adding new activities to their full professional schedules, and they inevitably have many questions about whether to become involved in peer review or in writing a course portfolio. Most faculty members are already quite busy, so it is reasonable to consider whether to allocate time to peer review of teaching. The leaders in an institution seeking to promote the peer review of teaching must anticipate and address the concerns of faculty. In the course of our project, we encountered many faculty members' questions and concerns, and we offer the following practical advice for addressing some of them.

Peer Review of Teaching Will Take Too Much of My Time.

Many faculty members simply believe that extra work on teaching takes too much time, and that that is a good enough reason to avoid considering it. There is no doubt about it: Writing and putting together a course portfolio will take time. But the teacher is not starting from scratch when writing a course portfolio. Most parts of a portfolio relate to issues that have already been resolved or materials already developed in designing and teaching any course. In addition, writing about a course either before or while that course is taught can bring to the surface issues in the design of classroom activities and assessment strategies that can then be modified before they cause problems with student learning. In our experience, when a teacher documents classroom goals, classroom methods, and the resulting student learning, he or she spends far less time making changes to subsequent offerings of that course. As such, the upfront expenditure of time typically has a large payoff in the professional work of a teacher. Also, in our experience, once a faculty member has gone through the process of writing a course portfolio, the inquiry process in teaching will never be the same. Even if they do not write another course portfolio, these teachers inevitably ask questions about their teaching in a more reflective and systematic way, thereby improving all of their future teaching.

Will My Work Really Be Used?

Students sometimes ask, "Will this be on the test?" implying they will try to learn only those things that are required or that are given grades. While we as teachers often lament this attitude in students, a version of this question pops up around peer review and other serious work on teaching: "This work will not be rewarded with promotion or merit in my department," or, "My campus does not care about teaching, only research." In contrast, many dedicated teachers view teaching as a noble calling and privilege and thus do not relish documenting their practices for the rough-and-tumble fight over resources during annual merit and promotion meetings. Our experience has led us to believe that reflective analysis of student understanding and conversation with colleagues results in improved teaching. Seeing this work, an intellectually curious teacher will want to include such collaboration within whatever window of time is available for work on teaching, even if it is not "on the test." Moreover, as both this chapter and Chapter 6 have described, engaging in peer review of teaching with colleagues often has powerful effects beyond the assessment of one's individual teaching. When faculty collaborate on making their teaching visible, either within departments or with colleagues across a campus, they have opportunities to shape and create improved campus climates for teaching. And instructors often feel reinvigorated about their teaching as a result.

Teaching Is an Art.

Some people believe teaching is an art that, ironically, cannot be taught. For them, reflecting on teaching processes is unnecessary because teaching is viewed as a performance that comes naturally through intuitive engagement with students. For them, uncovering the mechanics of what constitutes excellent teaching is at best unnecessary, and in the worst case could disrupt the rapport and flow of interaction among students, teachers, and content that they believe is the heart of good teaching. Our model of peer review does not take a position one way or another on the value of intensely personal, intuitive teaching; we do not prescribe any methods of teaching, and we understand that effective practice will likely vary widely by discipline and by institution. We do expect all teachers, however, to identify for themselves and for their students the characteristics of good performance, measured in their own terms. Once the teacher sets his or her goals for student understanding, it is reasonable to expect that, regardless of method, he or she will ask how many students achieve those goals. Whether by art or by formulaic instructional design, the point of the course is that students will learn. All instructors can reflect upon how their chosen approach to teaching helps them achieve the goals they have identified.

I Have Academic Freedom.

Many faculty members ask, "Doesn't academic freedom protect me from having to tell others what I'm doing in the classroom? Isn't teaching just between my students and me?" While academic freedom gives a teacher certain rights and protects a teacher's free speech as it pertains to research, academic freedom does not allow a teacher to neglect professional teaching duties.

Teaching is typically done within an educational community. For instance, at most schools course topics are approved through a series of curriculum committees. The faculty as a whole has set out curriculum goals and guidelines, and rarely is a single teacher responsible for defining an entire area of intellectual life on a campus. The community also takes responsibility for sustaining the resources needed to offer education at all, so there is an implicit agreement to contribute to commonly understood goals. Teachers cannot substitute and discard classroom topics without good reason, and colleagues have a vested interest in the success that one another's students have in achieving the goals the department or campus has collectively set for learning. Making teaching practices open for review and commentary by peers enables faculty members to demonstrate how they plan and deliver instruction in a variety of ways to facilitate students' proficiency in agreed-upon content and skills.

Student Learning Is Not My Responsibility.

An important question about our model of peer review addresses the focus on student learning as the primary topic of conversation. Many teachers recite one or many of the following: "I can't be held accountable if my students don't study"; "The high schools are terrible"; "The students work and have no time to do the reading or homework"; "Thursday night is now a drinking night."

Most of these statements are quite possibly true, and we, as teachers, do not control many aspects of our students' learning. But in order to maximize those areas of our students' learning that we do control, we need to collect and document some key information. For example, does the homework assigned in a class contribute to students' performance on their exams? Is there a relation between how well students do on out-of-class assignments and their in-class performance? Can the instructor document student improvement over a sequence of projects? Is the quality of learning for current students better than it was for those who took the class two years ago? What has been done to facilitate this improvement? Have students become so successful that the intellectual bar in a course can be raised? These are examples of areas where a teacher has some influence, regardless of the population of students who come in the door, and creating a course portfolio provides a method for inquiring into these questions for improved teacher practice. No one expects any educational process to yield perfect understanding in all students. It is fair, however, to expect teaching practices to be maximally up to date and well informed by contemporary standards so the resulting student understanding is as remarkable as it can be under the prevailing circumstances. Dealing with disadvantaged students in a challenged institutional setting is not acceptable grounds for indifferent performance as a teacher.

We answer many of these sincere questions from faculty members by reiterating our basic premise. We define an excellent teacher as one who is engaged in a well-prepared and intentional ongoing investigation of the best ways to promote a deep understanding on the part of as many students as possible. Excellent teaching is an integrated set of challenging activities that is comparable in difficulty to much of the research that we do (Bernstein, 2002). Toward this end, we believe that teachers need to make visible their intellectual work of teaching, using processes that parallel those used to explore a research question or creative project. Our work provides a model of how faculty members can make those results accessible for use, review, and assessment by their peers.

National Issues in Peer Review

Campus leaders should also know how the development of course portfolios and peer review fit into a larger national conversation about higher education. Some actions in support of better learning through better teaching can take place on an institutional level; solutions or remedies can be initiated through good local leadership, bits of policy adjustment, and occasional material support for programs. Other issues involve policies or values that are larger than any individual institution and may require a different level of analysis for proper consideration. We have found that we can support faculty interactions around teaching without addressing all these issues directly, but the continued development of peer review will certainly be affected by how these issues play out in the national conversation on teaching in higher education.

Including Course Portfolios in the Scholarship of Teaching and Learning

Being a coherent document in its own right, a course portfolio can be readily shared with other teachers through private exchange or public posting. The Peer Review of Teaching Project web site (www.courseportfolio.org) makes many course portfolios accessible to readers everywhere, and other projects around the world are also making integrated teaching work public (the Carnegie Academy for the Scholarship of Teaching and Learning and the Visible Knowledge Project are two notable examples). By its basic components, the course portfolio matches the characteristics of scholarship that Glassick, Huber, and Maeroff (1997) describe: Each course portfolio is a public, reflective document that reports sustained inquiry into the effectiveness of teaching practices in achieving intellectual goals. By being public, course portfolios also meet Shulman's (1999) proposed requirements for scholarship: Scholarship should be publicly accessible so that it can be reviewed critically by peers, built upon by others inquiring into the same issues, and used for improvement by practitioners of the same craft. Despite meeting these two well-received criteria for scholarship, the idea of public course portfolios still generates much discussion about whether it represents scholarship of teaching or stands only as an example of scholarly teaching (Richlin, 2001).

Boyer's (1990) division of academic work into four categories of scholarship has generated 16 years of valuable discussion about intellectual work, and his consideration of the scholarship of teaching has received the most attention in academic circles. Many writers such as Richlin (2001) draw a distinction between teaching that is done in the spirit of inquiry into learning and research on teaching that informs the professional community of educational scholars. In practice, and drawing upon the need for communication articulated by Glassick et al. (1997) in their account of the practices of scholars, many professionals argue that only published writing on teaching can qualify as scholarship.

The personnel policies of many academic institutions further highlight this distinction. These communities put such heavy emphasis on peer-reviewed publication that they will only accept published work as evidence of anything to be called *scholarship*. All other intellectual products related to teaching, even those that represent substantial inquiry into student learning, are put into a subordinate category called *scholarly teaching*. Although scholarly teaching is a desirable activity by all accounts, it is not widely promoted as the equal of its published cousins—journal articles, chapters, and books about teaching and learning. Most personnel systems do not recognize these scholarly activities as examples of scholarship, and accordingly the number of outlets for published reflective writing on teaching and learning is growing.

The course portfolios generated by Nebraska faculty members would appear to pose a problem for this emerging convention that relies on traditional publication as a defining characteristic of real scholarship. The work in the course portfolios includes all of the elements identified by Glassick et al. (1997) that characterize the actions of scholars, and the public web site makes the portfolios widely accessible to readers everywhere. Since they are accessible, the course portfolios can be subjected to review, comment, or criticism by peers of all kinds. Other teachers can use the insights they contain to enhance teaching and can build upon those insights to advance their own inquiry to new levels of sophistication. In that sense, course portfolios also meet Shulman's (1999) three criteria for scholarship. The barrier to acceptance of these portfolios as legitimate scholarship is really found in the unchanging traditions of academic institutions of many kinds. Since committees of senior faculty members often will not vote for tenure or promotion for younger colleagues whose work is not in print, the emerging scholarly teaching community is rushing to find outlets that meet the traditional criteria.

It seems somewhat ironic that these progressive scholars have agreed so willingly to internalize the standards of their senior colleagues by committing their findings to paper. Virtually everyone connected with the scholarship of teaching community cites Boyer's (1990) monograph, *Scholarship Reconsidered: Priorities of the Professoriate,* and the term *scholarship of teaching* comes from that work. A close reading of Boyer's writing, however, reveals his worry that increased attention to publication of research was taking valuable time and energy away from teaching per se. It was probably not his intent that our community turn all teachers into published scholars of educational research.

The fully accessible course portfolio may provide a convenient middle ground that will be most appropriate for a wide range of postsecondary teachers. Reading course portfolios can provide the background and context for high-quality conversations about learning and optimal practices in teaching. Whether informal interactions among teachers in one community or formal written reviews by independent readers from other schools, the substance of scholarly dialogue can be sustained using these representations of the intentional work of teachers and students. We believe our model provides an example of scholarship that will improve the learning that results from students' participation in our institutions. We are not proposing this work as a substitute for educational research done by professionals in schools of education. We do assert that representing the reflective practice of teachers will enhance the quality of the intellectual lives of faculty members, and that an institution would be very wise to promote, honor, and reward these activities—by whatever name.

The Peer Review of Teaching and Other National Communities

Our peer review project emerged from interactions among several national communities, and it is useful to situate the current state of our work within the larger view of higher education associations and groups.

Carnegie Foundation for the Advancement of Teaching

Probably the most central community is that which connects through the activities of the Carnegie Foundation for the Advancement of Teaching. The

Carnegie Academy for the Scholarship of Teaching and Learning (CASTL) is an umbrella organization that coordinates and connects activities by individual teachers and campuses who are interested in sharing work on student learning. Individual participants in both higher education and K–12 programs at CASTL are encouraged to use electronic course portfolios and posters to make their work visible to colleagues, and the campus program of CASTL promotes the use of portfolios to represent the work of larger units. Through its CASTL program, the Carnegie Foundation promotes the scholarship of teaching and learning in many forms, and its leaders have generously supported projects and groups of many kinds.

In addition to our project, which grew directly out of our participation in Carnegie-led initiatives, there is also the Visible Knowledge Project (VKP) based at Georgetown University's Center for New Designs in Learning and Scholarship. VKP also has a large and richly developed collection of electronic portfolios, mostly based in humanities courses. The overriding agenda of VKP is to promote advanced thinking by students through the use of teaching methods known as cognitive apprenticeship and scaffolding of learning. The electronic intellectual products at CASTL, VKP, and our Peer Review of Teaching Project share a strong similarity, and we are currently developing a common digital repository of portfolios produced by faculty working in these initiatives. The characteristics of this combined digital resource are still being formed, but we hope it will provide a readily accessible and searchable collection of ideas and learning products from higher education teaching.

One byproduct of the CASTL programs has been the emergence of a new organization, the International Society for the Scholarship of Teaching and Learning (ISSoTL). This organization was founded in 2004 by a large group of faculty members from the United States, Canada, the United Kingdom, and Australasia who had participated in various Carnegie programs. These leaders could see that CASTL would not be able to sustain indefinitely the level of activity that captured their interest and attention, and it was time for the scholars who have benefited from Carnegie's leadership to create an organization to carry on the idea. The first order of business for ISSoTL was to organize a conference for the annual sharing of scholarly teaching, and it was expressly modeled after an annual gathering called the Carnegie Colloquium. The organization has so far planned annual meetings through 2008, and it is organizing itself to be the professional home of scholars from many disciplines who wish to continue the excellent interaction they have found in various Carnegie Foundation–sponsored programs and events.

There is also a growing connection between these Carnegie-related communities and the Professional and Organizational Development Network (POD), an international organization of people who work in centers for teaching. The two communities have operated somewhat independently of each other, but there is an emerging recognition of a shared agenda and a shared interest in portfolios of learning. The activities of POD members have focused on the promotion of excellence in teaching, along with service to local educational institutions. A typical POD member is likely to be an organizer of events for higher education teachers, in a manner similar to the Carnegie leadership but in the context of a single institution. Relatively few faculty members participate in POD regional and national conferences. In that sense, POD is a complement to ISSoTL, which is more faculty-centered; the two organizations have common goals but approach the initiation of their work from different parts of each local institution. In addition, a large percentage of POD members have formal preparation in the field of education, typically with an advanced degree. That orientation to professional research has been aligned more with the notion that the scholarship of teaching and learning should look like educational research. In contrast, while the ISSoTL community has a representative number of participants from schools of education, the large majority of its members come from many academic disciplines. Because ISSoTL members are not in general professionally prepared to conduct social science research in the field of education, their contributions will come largely from their deep understanding of their own field of study.

Disciplinary Associations

Additional participation in this community comes from leaders in many disciplinary societies. Continued collaboration with those groups will be essential for peer review of teaching to succeed as a regular part of faculty life. For most higher education faculty members, a primary professional identity comes from the department that granted the Ph.D. As a young scholar moves around in different positions, the constant connection with the primary discipline is a defining element in the formation of professional attitudes and values. In most fields, one or perhaps two organizations coordinate activities shared by researchers, teachers, and practitioners in that field. These organizations often provide the major vehicles for scholarly communication by publishing journals within their field. As Huber and Morreale (2002) note, the style of intellectual work within each field will (and should) influence the form and the substance of scholarly activity related to the teaching of that field. It makes sense that faculty members would seek guidelines for scholarly work in the organizations that preserve those traditions of evidence and distribution of knowledge.

Increasingly, many disciplinary societies are now looking to integrate discussions about and research into teaching within their established conversations. Some disciplinary societies have directorates or divisions devoted to the teaching of their field, and many sponsor journals devoted to the teaching of particular fields. In this way, the highly valued and credible communities that already exist will shape the standards of process and the criteria for quality for peer review of teaching.

To our knowledge, these societies continue to rely on conventional print-based scholarly publication as the primary means of articulating the collective values of their membership around teaching excellence. Many people who are familiar with course portfolios (electronic and print) are working to develop collaborative relations with disciplinary societies in the hope of setting up some way of reviewing teaching materials that could reflect a deeper examination of the quality of teaching and learning. Existing boards of editors of discipline-based teaching journals would be a key source of potential reviewers for course portfolios. Many faculty members will value an activity only when they see it promoted, encouraged, and honored by their own disciplinary societies. Nurturing close ties with the leadership of disciplinary organizations will, over the long term, greatly aid in establishing peer-reviewed course portfolios as accepted scholarly practice.

It seems clear that peer collaboration in the development of formal representations of teaching and learning is at the heart of teaching activities in many national communities. Each of these groups is working hard to make quality work in learning and teaching visible. Their audiences are local colleagues, national communities, and institutional leaders who make important decisions about the careers of faculty members. Many of the long-term participants in this conversation, especially at the Carnegie Foundation, are fostering conversations among these different communities to forge a commonly shared vision and a public arena for continued support of intentional and reflective teaching. We believe that the methods and products of the Peer Review of Teaching Project provide a valuable resource for this emerging national community.

Ethical and Intellectual Property Issues

One consequence of keeping teaching behind closed doors all these years is the lack of circulation of intellectual products of teaching—lectures, assignments, class time activities, designs for hands-on activities, and systems for evaluating student understanding. Generally, no one but the teacher and students look at teaching materials, although some colleagues have shared their work on an informal basis. With the development of electronic course portfolios, the rich ideas, useful procedures, and effective materials created in courses are now visible to many other teachers, but our community does not have a well-established culture of appropriate citation when teaching ideas are borrowed or adapted.

One level of the issue is not very problematic, and that is the adaptation of others' insights or procedures into the teaching of a course. Since most of the time, teachers are not taking explicit professional credit for the details of how each class period unfolds, nothing would be "stolen" or misrepresented. Perhaps the teacher could mention in a syllabus or in class the source of a particular idea for an activity or an assignment, but the audience of students is not very tuned in to the community of creative instructional designers. Even in this case, however, we have seen professors who worry that they are committing some form of plagiarism by taking an idea from a course portfolio and working it into their own course. Such intellectual honesty is very refreshing to see, and we encourage them to acknowledge to their students (and any relevant colleagues) the source of their teaching practices or innovations. Perhaps we will see the development of community expectations for citation in course design, as we now routinely expect citation in discussions of research.

With the increasing desire to publish work about teaching, however, an emerging issue needs attention. One can imagine a professor placing some well-crafted materials and procedures in an open electronic course portfolio, only to find those materials published a year later by someone else, without attribution. We do not worry so much that faculty members will be intentionally dishonest in these actions; rather we are all operating in a new intellectual environment that does not have widely agreed-upon traditions and conventions about citation. One of the topics that the new organization ISSoTL might consider discussing is the establishment of guidelines for fair use of teaching ideas and materials, along with clear expectations about the nature and venue for citation of teaching work that is adapted for a different course. At the very least, we believe that taking creative credit for other people's work is never appropriate. The best format for identifying the source of ideas that have been broadly adapted to a different course in a different field of study may be more difficult to frame.

Building a Partnership Around Institutional Review Boards

Imagine a community of universities in which teaching is taken seriously and learning is well represented in descriptions of teaching: A large quantity of student work will be copied, scanned, and made visible for readers. Whether in course portfolios like ours or in any other format, thoughtful participants in the conversations around higher education will be looking at a great deal of intellectual work created by students. It seems wasteful of human time to have many members of campus IRBs looking individually at the lengthy applications of many, many teachers who plan to save, analyze, and reflect on their students' course performances.

The IRBs, a system of approval for this newly designated body of research on human subjects, was built to assure society that no harm would come to human beings as a result of inquiry brought by medical and social science researchers. Accordingly, that system is very detailed and has many checks and balances built into it, along with requirements for extensive preparation in ethical issues for all these researchers. Teachers will spend a lot of time preparing documentation about the way they will teach and how they will treat and safeguard all the materials they gather. Such an administrative burden will likely suppress the number of faculty members who would be willing to treat their own teaching as a form of inquiry into learning.

As we promote the idea of course portfolios as a tool for every faculty member in carrying out professionally responsible teaching, we hope that the system of research ethics management will recognize the need for treating this work differently. The safeguards and protections and documentation needed when psychologists ask families for permission to do untested interventions on their children, for example, are not appropriate for the study of teaching and learning, but many IRBs are not well set up to differentiate among applications for review, even for work in the "exempt" category.

A first step for academic leaders at any institution would be to work with the local IRB committees as they learn about this new breed of work called scholarship of teaching and learning. Ethical issues of privacy, ownership, and informed consent certainly need to be considered, but the risks and the complexity of the issues are rather modest and call only for some creativity in streamlining procedures. It may also be possible to aggregate the work of many investigators into a single application, allowing teachers in similar courses or units to address comparable questions in a single review. This move would save time for the IRB members and make it more likely that many faculty members would be willing to make their students' intellectual products visible for conversation. In a large vision, one might even consider the institution itself to be the principal investigator, filing a single massive IRB request for use of student work with permission. Such an act might help make teaching in general more ethical, while also enhancing faculty members' awareness of the importance of documenting and examining learning.

Indeed, arranging such ethical review across a campus would be very helpful to faculty who take teaching seriously. As local examples are created and become successful, it would be good for those institutions to share their experience with others. At that point, we hope, organizations like ISSoTL or the Carnegie Foundation might convene a larger national conversation with appropriate federal officials to identify local solutions that meet all of the ethical concerns needed while not weighing down the institution so much that its members become unwilling to examine archives of student work. Creative and effective local solutions can be held out as models for others.

We see this as an important issue because it is the direct examination of student work and consideration of the evaluation of that work that distinguishes our peer review model and its intellectual ancestors. Institutions have looked at content of teaching for as long as there have been curriculum committees, and letters from the back of the class and books on teaching tips have previously identified more and less successful approaches to classroom teaching. What has made this wave of peer review different and challenging is the inclusion of student performance at the heart of the process. If the ethical gathering of that evidence becomes mired in unnecessary administrative tasks, then the potential benefits of peer review of teaching will be greatly weakened. We believe that it will be possible to find streamlined procedures that will resurrect the original intent of making this work exempt from unnecessary regulation.

What's Next: Our Invitation to the Peer Review of Teaching

Through the continued practice of course portfolio development and peer review of the intellectual work in teaching, many practical and philosophical questions are being resolved. In the meantime, institutions need leaders who will guide local activity, support it with recognition and time, and connect it with teaching communities outside their campuses. These leaders also need to be ready to consider questions about the place of peer review in the larger domain of the scholarship of teaching. With so many different kinds of academic jobs, it is likely that many forms of work and forms of representation will exist side by side.

Campus leaders also need to understand the various reasons for which faculty members will be drawn to the peer review of teaching. Some faculty members will warmly embrace the opportunity to engage in research on their teaching, welcoming the tools and language of social science to do that work. Other faculty members will want to be effective and responsible teachers, desiring to engage in iterative reflection on the results of their own classes to keep their teaching on course. Others will be less enthusiastic and some may not engage at all; campus leaders will need to understand faculty's reasons for not participating but continue to keep the invitation open.

We believe that many faculty members will welcome our model of making teaching visible. In our experience at the University of Nebraska–Lincoln, the opportunity to interact with colleagues about teaching has been embraced by many faculty members. Our project has made significant progress in maximizing the likelihood that a faculty member will document and reflect upon the learning and understanding shown by students in a class. We believe that the process we have pioneered can be adapted for use by members of any academic community.

BIBLIOGRAPHY

Angelo, T. A., & Cross, K. P. (1993). *Classroom assessment techniques: A handbook for college teachers* (2nd ed.). San Francisco, CA: Jossey-Bass.

Bass, R. (1999, February). The scholarship of teaching: What's the problem? *Inventio, 1*(1). Retrieved January 16, 2006, from www.doit.gmu.edu/Archives/feb98/randybass.htm

Bernstein, D., & Wert, E. (2004). Making visible the intellectual work in teaching. *Tomorrow's Professor Msg. #554.* Retrieved January 16, 2006, from http://ctl.stanford.edu/Tomprof/postings/554.html

Bernstein, D. J. (1996). A departmental system for balancing the development and evaluation of college teaching: A commentary on Cavanagh. *Innovative Higher Education, 20*(4), 241–247.

Bernstein, D. J. (2002). Representing the intellectual work in teaching through peer-reviewed course portfolios. In S. F. Davis & W. Buskist (Eds.), *The teaching of psychology: Essays in honor of Wilbert J. McKeachie and Charles L. Brewer* (pp. 215–229). Mahwah, NJ: Lawrence Erlbaum.

Bernstein, D. J., Jonson, J., & Smith, K. (2000). An examination of the implementation of peer review of teaching. In K. E. Ryan (Ed.), *New directions for teaching and learning: No. 83. Evaluating teaching in higher education: A vision for the future* (pp. 73–85). San Francisco, CA: Jossey-Bass.

Boyer, E. L. (1990). *Scholarship reconsidered: Priorities of the professoriate.* Princeton, NJ: Carnegie Foundation for the Advancement of Teaching.

Brookfield, S. D. (1995). *Becoming a critically reflective teacher.* San Francisco, CA: Jossey-Bass.

Centra, J. A. (1993). *Reflective faculty evaluation: Enhancing teaching and determining faculty effectiveness.* San Francisco, CA: Jossey-Bass.

Cerbin, W. (1994). The course portfolio as a tool for continuous improvement of teaching and learning. *Journal on Excellence in College Teaching, 5*(1), 95–105.

Chism, N. V. N. (1999). *Peer review of teaching: A sourcebook.* Bolton, MA: Anker.

Davis, B. G. (1993). *Tools for teaching.* San Francisco, CA: Jossey-Bass.

Edgerton, R., Hutchings, P., & Quinlan, K. (1991). *The teaching portfolio: Capturing the scholarship in teaching.* Washington, DC: American Association for Higher Education.

Fink, L. D. (2003). *Creating significant learning experiences: An integrated approach to designing college courses.* San Francisco, CA: Jossey-Bass.

Glassick, C. E., Huber, M. T., & Maeroff, G. I. (1997). *Scholarship assessed: Evaluation of the professoriate.* San Francisco, CA: Jossey-Bass.

Huber, M. T., & Morreale, S. P. (Eds.). (2002). *Disciplinary styles in the scholarship of teaching and learning: Exploring common ground.* Washington, DC: American Association for Higher Education.

Hutchings, P. (1993). *Using cases to improve college teaching: A guide to more reflective practice.* Washington, DC: American Association for Higher Education.

Hutchings, P. (Ed.). (1995). *From idea to prototype: The peer review of teaching.* Washington, DC: American Association for Higher Education.

Hutchings, P. (1996). *Making teaching community property: A menu for peer collaboration and peer review.* Washington, DC: American Association for Higher Education.

Hutchings, P. (Ed.). (1998). *The course portfolio: How faculty can examine their teaching to advance practice and improve student learning.* Washington, DC: American Association for Higher Education.

Hutchings, P. (Ed.). (2000). *Opening lines: Approaches to the scholarship of teaching and learning.* Menlo Park, CA: Carnegie Foundation for the Advancement of Teaching.

Hutchings, P. (Ed.). (2002). *Ethics of inquiry: Issues in the scholarship of teaching and learning.* Menlo Park, CA: Carnegie Foundation for the Advancement of Teaching.

Marshall, M. J. (2004). *Response to reform: Composition and the professionalization of teaching.* Carbondale, IL: Southern Illinois University Press.

McKeachie, W. J. (2001). *McKeachie's teaching tips: Strategies, research, and theory for college and university teachers* (11th ed.). Boston, MA: Houghton Mifflin.

Richlin, L. (2001). Scholarly teaching and the scholarship of teaching. In C. Kreber (Ed.), *New directions for teaching learning: No. 86. Scholarship revisited: Perspectives on the scholarship of teaching* (pp. 57–67). San Francisco, CA: Jossey-Bass.

Salvatori, M. R. (2000). Difficulty: The great educational divide. In P. Hutchings (Ed.), *Opening lines: Approaches to the scholarship of teaching and learning* (pp. 81–94). Menlo Park, CA: Carnegie Foundation for the Advancement of Teaching.

Shulman, L. S. (1999, July/August). Taking learning seriously. *Change, 31*(4), 10–17.

Stcarns, P. N., Seixas, P., & Wineburg, S. (Eds.). (2000). *Knowing, teaching and learning history: National and international perspectives.* New York, NY: New York University Press.

Walvoord, B. E., & Anderson, V. J. (1998). *Effective grading: A tool for learning and assessment.* San Francisco, CA: Jossey-Bass.

Wergin, J. F. (2005a, January/February). Taking responsibility for student learning: The role of accreditation. *Change, 37*(1), 30–33.

Wergin, J. F. (2005b, May/June). Higher education: Waking up to the importance of accreditation. *Change, 37*(3), 35–41.

Wiggins, G., & McTighe, J. (2001). *Understanding by design.* Upper Saddle River, NJ: Prentice Hall.

Wineburg, S. (2001). *Historical thinking and other unnatural acts: Charting the future of teaching the past.* Philadelphia, PA: Temple University Press.

Index